People and Parks

Linking Protected Area Management with Local Communities

Michael Wells and Katrina Brandon

with Lee Hannah

The World Bank • *The World Wildlife Fund* • *U.S. Agency for International Development*

Washington, D.C.

The findings, interpretations, and conclusions expressed in this paper are entirely those of the authors and should not be attributed in any manner to the World Bank, to its affiliated organizations, or to members of its Board of Executive Directors or the countries they represent; to the World Wildlife Fund; or to the U.S. Agency for International Development. The boundaries, colors, denominations, and other information shown on any map in this volume do not imply on the part of the World Bank Group any judgment on the legal status of any territory or the endorsement or acceptance of such boundaries.

The material in this publication is copyrighted. Requests for permission to reproduce portions of it should be sent to the Office of the Publisher at the address shown in the copyright notice above. The World Bank encourages dissemination of its work and will normally give permission promptly and, when the reproduction is for noncommercial purposes, without asking a fee. Permission to copy portions for classroom use is granted through the Copyright Clearance Center, Inc., Suite 910, 222 Rosewood Drive, Danvers, Massachusetts 01923, U.S.A.

The complete backlist of publications from the World Bank is shown in the annual *Index of Publications*, which contains an alphabetical title list (with full ordering information) and indexes of subjects, authors, and countries and regions. The latest edition is available free of charge from the Distribution Unit, Office of the Publisher, The World Bank, 1818 H Street, N.W., Washington, D.C. 20433, U.S.A., or from Publications, The World Bank, 66, avenue d'Iéna, 75116 Paris, France.

At the time of writing, Michael Wells was a consultant to the Policy and Research Division of the World Bank's Environment Department, Katrina Brandon was with the Wildlands and Human Needs Program of the World Wildlife Fund-U.S., and Lee Hannah was with the Africa Bureau of the U.S. Agency for International Development. Currently, Michael Wells remains a consultant to the same division in the Bank, Katrina Brandon is a senior fellow with World Wildlife Fund-U.S. and a consultant to the Policy and Research Division of the World Bank's Environment Department, and Lee Hannah is the Philippines and Madagascar Program Adviser with Conservation International.

Library of Congress Cataloging-in-Publication Data

Wells, Michael, 1954–
   People and parks : linking protected area management with local
communities / Michael Wells and Katrina Brandon, with Lee Hannah.
     p. cm.
   Includes bibliographical references.
   ISBN 0-8213-2053-X
   1. National parks and reserves—Management—Citizen participation.
   2. Natural areas—Management—Citizen participation.
   3. Conservation of natural resources—Citizen participation.
   4. Economic development projects—Management—Citizen participation.
   I. Brandon, Katrina, 1957–   . II. Hannah, Lee Jay. III. Title.
SB486.M35W45   1992
333.78'091724—dc20
                                                  92-134
                                               CIP

Contents

Maps

Foreword

Conserving biological diversity has emerged as a priority shared by both conservation and development organizations. While parks and protected areas have been the traditional approach to conservation, many protected areas are rapidly becoming "islands" as the wildlands around them are converted to alternative, often incompatible, uses. In the face of relentless human pressures, enforcement alone will not preserve these areas. Conservation thus requires a perspective that stretches well beyond park boundaries and involves national policies as well as programs affecting rural communities.

New approaches to protected area management that integrate the needs of local people while conserving natural resources have increasingly been initiated over the past decade. Such projects, introduced in this report as integrated conservation-development projects (ICDPs), combine the most difficult aspects of rural development and of conservation. The common objective of ICDPs is to link the conservation of biological diversity in protected areas with local social and economic development.

The World Bank, the World Wildlife Fund, and the U.S. Agency for International Development initiated this study to assess the early experiences of ICDPs. Michael Wells, Katrina Brandon, and their colleagues have examined twenty-three of the most widely acclaimed ICDPs in what is—as far as we know—the most rigorous analysis of this approach undertaken so far. The results are sobering but encouraging. Although progress has been modest in many areas, this is partly attributable to financial constraints and to the lack of experience of the participating organizations.

This study lays the groundwork for providing the World Bank, the World Wildlife Fund, the U.S. Agency for International Development, and other agencies with information about what is needed to develop and implement ICDPs in the future. It highlights the critical importance of launching projects in a supportive policy environment and makes specific recommendations for future project design and implementation. The authors also emphasize the need for a mix of organizations with complementary skills and resources—including development agencies and nongovernmental organizations—to work together with governments and local people in the design and implementation of ICDPs.

If we are to preserve biodiversity in parks and protected areas, the challenge before us is to build on the lessons of *People and Parks* and truly learn how to link protected area management with local communities.

Mohammed T. El-Ashry
Director
Environment Department
The World Bank

R. Michael Wright
Senior Vice President
Developing Countries Program
The World Wildlife Fund

Jerry Wólgin
Acting Director
Office of Analysis, Research, and
  Technical Support, Africa Bureau
United States Agency for
  International Development

Acknowledgments

We owe our largest debt to the people living in and around protected areas who generously contributed their time and expertise in response to our inquiries, together with field staff of our case study projects and employees of government conservation agencies.

The study was directed by John Spears and Mohan Munasinghe for the World Bank and by Michael Wright for World Wildlife Fund-U.S. Gloria Davis provided helpful ideas and guidance throughout. Valuable discussions were also held with John Dixon, Mary Dyson, John English, Agnes Kiss, Russell Mittermeier, Jeff McNeely, Alison Richard, Jeff Sayer, Mingma Norbu Sherpa, and Jan Wind.

Michael Wells prepared the Indonesia, Madagascar, Nepal, Tanzania, and Thailand case studies. Katrina Brandon conducted the Costa Rica and Mexico case studies. Lee Hannah prepared the case studies for Burundi, Kenya, and Rwanda. Kent Elbow's visits to protected areas in Niger and Burkina Faso provided background for the case studies for those two countries. John J. Earhart and Robert Simeone prepared the case study on Central Selva, Peru. Michael Kiernan provided detailed information on the Boscosa project in Costa Rica, Central Selva in Peru, and the Pilot Forestry Plan in Mexico.

In addition to those already named, many others also commented on earlier drafts of the manuscript: Emmanuel Asibey, Greg Booth, Roland Bunch, Mac Chapin, Gary Cohen, Steve Cornelius, Charles Geisler, Nicole Glineur, Gary Hartshorn, Peter Hazelwood, David Hulse, Kevin Lyonette, William McLarney, Ridley Nelson, Samuel Paul, Mario Ramos, Colin Rees, Walt Reid, Frances Seymous, Alfredo Sfeir-Younis, Ted Smith, Pamela Stanbury, Roger Stone, Benjamin Stoner, Dwight Walker, Barbara Wyckoff-Baird, and Montague Yudelman.

Invaluable assistance was provided during site visits by Nieck Bech, Russell Betts, Teeka and Samita Bhattarai, Bruce Bunting, K.S. Depari, Richard Donovan, Suraphon Duangkae, Ketty Faichampa, Chandra Gurung, David Hulse, Jack Hurd, Bob Kakuyo, Joseph Lindi, Clark Lundgren, James Lynch, Robert Malpas, Nilamber Mishra, John Newby, Sheila O'Connor, Pisit na Patalung, Samson Rana, Alberto Salas, Andy Silcox, Tray Sinha, Anne-Marie Skjold, Wilas Techo, Biswanath Upreti, and David Western.

Excellent editorial and production support was provided by Meta de Coquereaumont, assisted by Jane Seegal (editor), Katrina Van Duyn (proofreader), and Mary Mahy (desktopper). The University of Maryland Cartographic Services Department, particularly Joseph School and David Nale, transformed cryptic sketches into maps.

Financial support was provided by the World Bank through the Norwegian Support to the Environment, the World Wildlife Fund-U.S., and the U.S. Agency for International Development.

Summary

National parks, wildlife reserves, and other types of protected areas are at the forefront of efforts to conserve biological diversity. But many protected areas are in crisis. Already underfunded, they have come under increasing pressure from the expanding scale of human activities outside—and sometimes inside—their boundaries. Conflicts of interest have thus arisen in many areas of the world between protected areas and local people. Traditional approaches to park management and enforcement activities have been unable to balance these competing objectives.

In response, a new set of initiatives, introduced here as integrated conservation-development projects (ICDPs), has been launched. These projects attempt to ensure the conservation of biological diversity by reconciling the management of protected areas with the social and economic needs of local people. The smaller ICDPs include biosphere reserves, multiple-use areas, and a variety of initiatives on the boundaries of protected areas, including buffer zones. Larger projects include the implementation of regional land use plans with protected area components, as well as large-scale development projects with links to nearby protected areas.

This study looks at the early experiences of twenty-three such projects in Africa, Asia, and Latin America. The report explores the social, ecological, technical, and institutional issues that arise from these attempts to link protected area management with local development. It identifies the vital elements in the design of ICDPs and assesses the effectiveness of field experience. Last, it elaborates lessons for future programs to conserve biodiversity in developing countries.

What are integrated conservation-development projects?

Understanding integrated conservation-development projects requires understanding the evolu-

tion in conservation thinking toward a greater emphasis on the broader societal role of protected areas and their potential contributions to sustainable development. Although the ICDP approach has been heavily publicized and is rapidly expanding its influence, assessment of activities to date has been limited. The twenty-three case study projects examined in this report were selected from among those that have been described as the most promising and effective (chapter 1).

The physical and ecological characteristics of the case study projects varied substantially, as did their management objectives and their relations with local people. Variability in the institutional influences—laws, policies, social changes, and economic forces—was also considerable. It was apparent that many of the projects had begun with only a very limited understanding of the root causes of the threats to the protected areas that they were attempting to conserve, threats that arose from complex social, economic, cultural, and political interactions (chapter 2). To provide more insight into this diversity—and the similarities as well—three case study projects, one in each region, and their accomplishments are examined in some detail (chapter 3).

Design and implementation issues

To achieve their objectives, ICDPs engage in three distinct types of operations. *Protected area management* activities include biological resource inventories and monitoring, patrols to prevent illegal activities, infrastructure maintenance, applied biological research, and conservation education. Some ICDPs try to establish *buffer zones* around protected areas. While the concept has strong intuitive appeal, there are many difficulties in trying to put it into practice, and actual working examples of buffer zones among the case study projects were virtually nonexistent. *Local social and economic development* activities constitute the third type of operation, and these use approaches that are comparable to those in rural development projects, or simpler approaches that rely on compensation and substitution strategies (chapter 4).

Efforts to promote social and economic development among communities adjacent to protected area boundaries represent the central concern of the ICDP approach and clearly distinguish it from other conservation approaches. Promoting local development is a highly complex and challenging task for conservation practitioners, and in this effort, many of the lessons from earlier rural development projects are applicable to ICDPs as well. To achieve their aims, ICDPs must ensure that the activities of their development components are consistent with the overall goal of conserving biodiversity. One of the most challenging tasks for ICDP managers is to promote development activities that not only improve local living standards but also lead to strengthened management of protected areas.

At a more general level, ICDPs need to challenge the widespread but unsupported assumption that people who are made better off as a result of a development project will refrain from illegal exploitation of a nearby protected area even in the absence of the negative incentive provided by more effective penalties. Such expectations appear naive, and the need to strengthen guard patrols and to impose penalties for illegal activities in protected areas remains strong. Enforcement activities are not inconsistent with the ICDP concept when they are integrated with genuine local development efforts and serious attempts to improve local people-park communications through educational campaigns and other means.

These complexities all reemphasize the importance of establishing *explicit linkages* between the different components of an ICDP. Many types of development activities have the potential for increasing local incomes and living standards. What is less clear is how such activities can be expected to enhance the conservation of biological diversity, particularly in the absence of more effective enforcement. In other words, very careful thought needs to be given at the design stage to the following question: what are the anticipated linkages between the planned realization of social and economic benefits by people living *outside* the park or reserve boundaries and the necessary behavioral response the project seeks to achieve to reduce pressure *inside* the boundaries (chapter 4)?

Attempts to generate local social and economic benefits through the development components of

ICDPs were concentrated in five areas: (1) natural resource management outside protected areas, particularly in agroforestry, forestry, irrigation and water control, and wildlife; (2) community social services, such as schools and health clinics; (3) nature tourism; (4) road construction for market access; and (5) direct employment generation.

The case study projects have resulted in numerous benefits for local people, principally through income gains and improved access to social services. From a strictly development perspective, several of the projects appear quite promising, and one or two of them quite successful. But in virtually all the projects, the critical linkage between development and conservation is either missing or obscure.

Thus it is questionable whether many of the project activities have generated local benefits that have reduced pressures on the parks or reserves they are trying to protect—the key objective of ICDPs (chapter 5).

Empowering local people

Involving local people in the process of change and development and enabling them to wisely manage the resource base is a necessary, but difficult, component of ICDPs. Few of the projects specified what they meant by local participation, and most have treated local people as passive beneficiaries rather than as active collaborators. Some ICDPs found it necessary to generate short-term benefits to establish credibility. But such immediate gains are not a substitute for the time-consuming and intensive process of involving communities in project design and implementation over the long term. Achieving a balance between the short- and long-term goals is essential, as is balancing participation with enforcement activities (chapter 6).

Participating organizations

The case study ICDPs were executed by a mix of government agencies, conservation and development nongovernmental organizations, and development agencies operating independently or in partnership. Nongovernmental organizations ranged from small local organizations to large international conservation groups, yet few had the capacity to design, implement, evaluate, or fund large ICDPs. Government agencies often lack adequate financial resources and personnel, and jurisdictional conflicts between agencies responsible for activities inside protected areas and those operating outside these areas were common. The nongovernmental organizations participating in ICDPs brought important strengths and experience in conservation but sometimes lacked the expertise needed to design, implement, or evaluate integrated projects with development components.

There is debate over whether ICDPs should be top-down or bottom-up in their design and implementation. Top-down tends to be associated with governments and international organizations, and bottom-up with nongovernmental organizations. The case studies revealed little convincing evidence that, working independently, governments, conservation organizations, or development organizations can effectively plan and implement ICDPs. Partnerships between conservation and development organizations and between these organizations and government agencies are proposed as essential for the success of ICDPs (chapter 7).

Measuring effectiveness

The ultimate objective of ICDPs is the conservation of biological diversity in parks and reserves. All ICDPs must eventually face the test of whether they have strengthened the ability of protected areas to conserve the species and ecosystems the areas were established to protect. It is possible for a project to have successful social and economic development components without being an effective ICDP.

The scale of projects was an important element in their effectiveness. For example, if a project works in only a few of the communities surrounding a protected area, its overall influence in protecting the park may be weak, even if the project's effectiveness in those communities is strong. Several other factors were also associated with improvements in biodiversity conservation at case study sites, including more effective enforcement, mitigation of the adverse impacts of tourism, specific agreements for local development, and direct linkage of conservation goals to development benefits (chapter 8).

Lessons

ICDPs cannot address the underlying threats to biological diversity. Many of the factors leading to the erosion of biodiversity and the degradation of protected natural ecosystems in developing countries originate far from park boundaries. Among them are public ownership of extensive areas of land unmatched by the capacity of government agencies to manage these lands; powerful financial incentives encouraging overexploitation of timber, wildlife, grazing lands, and crop fields; an absence of linkages between the needs of conservation and the factors encouraging development; and laws, policies, social changes, and economic forces over which poor people in remote rural areas have no influence.

Addressing these issues in a meaningful way would require engaging the highest levels of governments throughout the industrialized and developing worlds and mobilizing resources on a much larger scale than has been done so far. Today, even under the best of conditions, ICDPs centered on protected areas and directed to local populations can play only a modest role in mitigating the powerful forces causing environmental degradation.

In these circumstances, it is perhaps remarkable what the case study projects *have* managed to achieve. ICDPs are attempting to combine the most difficult aspects of conservation and park management with rural development. Despite formidable constraints, what many of this first generation of projects have achieved is significant. While traditional enforcement will continue to play a critical role—and in many cases needs desperately to be strengthened and expanded—it will have to be coupled in many instances with efforts to benefit local people. This means that innovative, well-designed ICDPs that constructively address local people-park relationships at carefully selected sites are an essential element in the conservation of biodiversity, and therefore of sustainable development efforts.

But for ICDPs to play a significant role in conserving biological diversity, decisive actions need to be taken by implementing organizations, by national governments, and by lenders and donors, including international development agencies. Without deliberate and concerted actions by these groups, the outlook for biodiversity will be bleak. The long gestation periods needed for ICDPs to produce results clearly means that these actions must be taken sooner rather than later. Recommendations for future ICDP initiatives are made in several categories: (1) projects as part of a larger framework that includes such preconditions as adequate political support, enabling legislation, realistic institutional arrangements, and compatibility with regional development, resource tenure, and institutional orientation; (2) scale of projects; (3) participating organizations; (4) site selection; (5) local participation; (6) financial resources; and (7) project design and implementation (chapter 9).

The challenge for the future is not just to design and implement more effective ICDPs. That will be feasible, although it will require more financial support, creative modifications of existing approaches, and application of a much more thorough understanding of the rural development process. The greater challenge will be to engage the individuals and organizations that have the capacity and the commitment to establish social, economic, legal, and institutional environments that facilitate rather than frustrate achievement of the ICDP goal of conserving biodiversity.

1. Rationale for a new approach

Protected areas—such as national parks and wildlife reserves—have long been recognized as playing a crucial role in conserving biological diversity. But many of these areas are at serious risk, partly because of the hardship they impose on members of local communities. Traditional approaches to park management have generally been unsympathetic to the constraints facing local people, relying on guard patrols and penalties to exclude local people. This study looks at new approaches to protected area management that are attempting to address the needs of nearby communities by emphasizing local participation and by combining conservation with development. We have coined the term "integrated conservation-development projects" (ICDPs) to refer to projects that use these approaches.

This study of twenty-three projects in Africa, Asia, and Latin America is intended to identify the lessons of the first few years of ICDP implementation, and the implications for future conservation policies, programs, and projects.

Background

The world's biological diversity is increasingly concentrated in the diminishing number of natural areas that have remained more or less unchanged by human activities (Wilson 1988). Biodiversity conservation efforts have concentrated on establishing networks of parks and reserves to protect these sites. As a result, many of the world's outstanding and most celebrated natural areas have been granted official conservation status through designation as a national park, wildlife reserve, or other protected category.

National parks originated in the United States in the nineteenth century. Boundaries were drawn around "special places" so they could be "set aside" from the "ravages" of ordinary use (Hales 1989, 140) for visitors' inspiration and enjoyment. The theme of protecting natural phenomena from exploitation for public enjoyment served as a model for the development of protected areas worldwide (Machlis and Tichnell 1985). Many parks were established—particularly in Africa and Asia—to protect the larger mammals that had captured the imagination of Europeans and North Americans and to attract international tourism (Hales 1989).

Although national parks are perhaps the best known, there are several other types of protected areas (table 1.1). Protected areas and parks that were established mainly to maintain biological diversity and natural formations are referred to as strictly protected areas (categories I to III). The remainder (categories IV to VIII) allow some degree of human use and controlled exploitation.

These management categories are based on various laws and regulations governing protected areas. But legal protection rarely translates into protected area security. Many of the most important protected areas are experiencing serious and increasing degradation as a result of large-scale development projects, expanding agricultural frontiers, illegal hunting and logging, fuelwood collection, and uncontrolled burning. If current trends continue, the biological diversity in many critical conservation areas will diminish dramatically in the next few decades.

Parks and people

Most protected areas were originally established with little or no regard for local people, few of whom could benefit from tourism. In fact, park management has emphasized a policing role aimed at excluding local people—sometimes characterized as the "fences and fines" approach. Machlis and Tichnell (1985, 96), among others, have argued that this "preservationist approach....requires an essentially militaristic defense strategy and will almost always heighten conflict."

Table 1.1 Protected area categories and management objectives

Category	Type	Objective
I	Scientific reserve/strict nature reserve	Protect nature and maintain natural processes in an undisturbed state. Emphasize scientific study, environmental monitoring and education, and maintenance of genetic resources in a dynamic and evolutionary state.
II	National park	Protect relatively large natural and scenic areas of national or international significance for scientific, educational, and recreational use.
III	Natural monument/natural landmark	Preserve nationally significant natural features and maintain their unique characteristics.
IV	Managed nature reserve/wildlife sanctuary	Protect nationally significant species, groups of species, biotic communities, or physical features of the environment when these require specific human manipulation for their perpetuation.
V	Protected landscapes	Maintain nationally significant natural landscapes characteristic of the harmonious interaction of people and land while providing opportunities for public recreation and tourism within the normal life-style and economic activity of these areas.
VI	Resource reserve	Protect natural resources for future use and prevent or contain development that could affect resources pending the establishment of management objectives based on appropriate knowledge and planning.
VII	Natural biotic area/ anthropological reserve	Allow societies to live in harmony with the environment, undisturbed by modern technology.
VIII	Multiple-use management area/ managed resource area	Sustain production of water, timber, wildlife, pasture, and outdoor recreation. Conservation of nature oriented to supporting economic activities (although specific zones can also be designed within these areas to achieve specific conservation objectives).

Source: International Union for Conservation of Nature and Natural Resources (IUCN 1985).

The conservation community has acknowledged that communities next to protected area boundaries frequently bear substantial costs—as a result of lost access—while receiving little in return. Local residents, who tend to be poor and receive few government services, often perceive protected areas as restricting their ability to earn a living. It is not surprising that the pressures of growing populations and unsustainable land use practices outside protected area boundaries frequently lead to illegal and destructive encroachment.

Reflecting these concerns, the 1980 *World Conservation Strategy*, a major document reflecting the views of numerous groups, emphasized the importance of linking protected area management with the economic activities of local communities (IUCN 1980). The need to include local people in protected area planning and management also was adopted enthusiastically by conservationists and protected area managers at the 1982 World Congress on National Parks, in Bali. This congress called for increased support for communities next to parks through such measures as education, revenue sharing, participation in decisions, appropriate development schemes near protected areas, and—where compatible with the protected areas' objectives—access to resources (McNeely and Miller 1984). More recently, growing awareness of the complexity of the links between poverty, development, and the environment has led to a search for ways to link conservation with development, make "sustainable development" work, and make conservation people-oriented (for example, World Commission 1987).

Recognition thus is growing that the successful long-term management of protected areas depends on the cooperation and support of local people, and that it is often neither politically feasible nor ethically justifiable to exclude the poor—who have limited access to resources—from parks and reserves without providing them alternative means of livelihood. This has led to increasing efforts by protected area managers and conservation organizations to obtain local cooperation, and to the introduction of ICDPs.

Integrated conservation-development projects

ICDPs vary considerably in scale and scope. The smaller projects include biosphere reserves, multiple-use areas, and initiatives on the boundaries of national parks, including buffer zones. Larger projects include both regional land use plans with protected area components and large-scale development projects with links to nearby protected areas. Most ICDPs aim to stabilize land use outside protected boundaries and to increase local incomes, in order to reduce the pressure for further exploitation of natural resources in the protected area. Many ICDPs also emphasize conservation education.

Efforts to link conservation and development have featured prominently in the discussion of sustainable development that has blossomed since the early 1980s. As a result, ICDPs have received considerable attention among conservation organizations, international development agencies, national governments, and private foundations. ICDPs have been funded or implemented by many of these organizations.

The World Bank's 1986 policy on wildlands—defined as natural areas relatively untouched by human activities—recognizes the importance of wildland management to development projects and requires that wildland management be considered in economic and sectoral planning (Ledec and Goodland 1988). The wildlands policy has resulted in increasing numbers of development projects with a conservation or protected area component. The policy emphasizes the need "to include local people in the planning and benefits [of wildland management areas]." It also notes that "rural development investments that provide farmers and villagers in the vicinity of [wildland management areas with] an alternative to further encroachment" can contribute to effective conservation in parks and reserves.

The World Wildlife Fund launched the Wildlands and Human Needs Program in 1985, with matching financial support from the U.S. Agency for International Development (USAID) and the Moriah Fund. This program consists of about twenty protected area projects in developing countries that have been planned to give equal emphasis to conservation and development. The program aims to use community development initiatives to minimize the impact of local people on significant wildland areas. It is an experimental program, the first of its type to be launched by a conservation organization. Several Wildlands and Human Needs Program projects were examined in this study.

Need for the study

Despite growing interest in the ICDP approach—and new and expanded funding sources—field experience is limited. There is little analytical literature in this area, and criteria for evaluating the projects have not yet been clearly identified. Many projects have barely proceeded beyond the planning stages, and the few advanced or completed projects have not been systematically examined. The extent to which investments in ICDPs are cost-effective, sustainable, or replicable approaches to protected area management and the conservation of biodiversity is thus still unknown.

An examination of ICDPs was considered important for several reasons. First, many developing countries are giving the conservation of biodiversity a more prominent position on their agendas. Policymakers thus are asking which approaches are appropriate and cost-effective. Second, the number of ICDPs being initiated has grown dramatically. It has become rare to find a forest or park management project proposal that does not talk about local community involvement, buffer zones, or other ICDP concepts. These and future projects should benefit from an evaluation of the experience to date. Finally, and perhaps most urgent, a failure to initiate and maintain more effective approaches to managing protected areas will result in the continued rapid decline of critical natural ecosystems. New and effective approaches need to be adopted in the 1990s to prevent substantial, possibly catastrophic, further losses in biological diversity.

Methodology

The study was based on site visits, supplemented by sources that included project proposals, progress reports, and evaluations. Whenever possible, discussions were held with past and present project managers and their staff, protected area managers and their staff, senior representatives of national agencies charged with protected area administration, senior staff of national nongovernmental organizations participating in the project, national staff of international nongovernmental organizations participating in the project, intended beneficiaries of the project development and education components, and other individuals in the countries with relevant knowledge.

Some of these discussions were in formal meetings, others in informal settings. Discussions with the intended beneficiaries of projects in Africa and Asia required interpreters; whenever possible, these discussions were informal and without project or government representatives present.

The agenda for the case study reviews was flexible and varied according to project scope and scale. It was recognized in advance that only limited quantitative information would be available on any project. The limited time available for site visits precluded collecting original data, which meant that most of the information collected was qualitative.

Approaches to community use of natural resources were excluded from the study if they did not include a protected area and did not have the conservation of biological diversity as their principal objective. Examples of such approaches include social forestry (see, for example, Gregersen, Draper, and Elz 1989) or extractive reserves (see, for example, World Wildlife Fund 1990). This study's scope is broader than the related work of Poole (1989), which was limited to the consideration of indigenous peoples living in conservation areas, principally in Latin America. Additional ICDP case studies may be found in the work of West and Brechin (1990), who also discuss protected areas in industrialized countries.

Selection of the case study sites

Candidate sites were identified through discussions with the staffs of the Asian Development Bank, CARE, Catholic Relief Services, Conservation International, Inter-American Foundation, USAID, U.S. Peace Corps, Wildlife Conservation International, World Bank, International Union for the Conservation of Nature and National Resources (IUCN), World Wildlife Fund, and other individuals with experience of developing country conservation and development issues.

Case study selection was limited to projects with social or economic development components linked to protected areas that had been implemented for at least three years as of late 1989. About thirty projects that satisfied these criteria were originally identified. Fewer than ten had been operating for more than six years. Final selections reflected a desire for representation from Africa, Asia, and Latin America. The choices also reflected a subjective assessment of what were felt to be the most interesting and varied projects, and the logistical feasibility of visiting and evaluating the projects during the study. Preference was given to eight countries where ICDPs had been initiated at more than one site. A small number of sites were included where some efforts had been made to improve local people-park relations without a specific project. Most site visits, usually for one to two weeks, were conducted between September 1989 and March 1990. Most sites were visited by one of the authors, although several sites were visited by others under supervision by the authors.

Brief descriptions of the projects at each case study site are included in box 1.1 and their locations are shown on map 1.1. Summaries describing and analyzing each case study, and site maps, are included in the appendix. Extended versions of these summaries are available from the authors.

Map 1.1 Case study sites

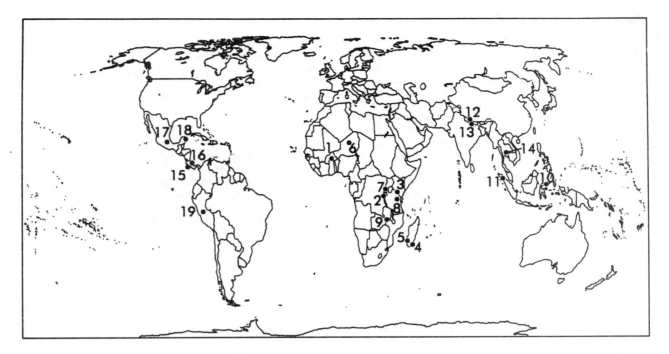

Africa

1. **Burkina Faso, Nazinga Game Ranch**
2. **Burundi, Bururi Forest Reserve and Rumonge, Vyanda, and Kigwena Reserves**
3. **Kenya, Amboseli National Park**
4. **Madascar, Andohahela Integral Reserve**
5. **Madagascar, Beza Mahafaly Special Reserve Area**
6. **Niger, Air-Tenere Nature Reserve**
7. **Rwanda, Volcanoes National Park**
8. **Tanzania, East Usambara Mountains**
9. **Zambia, Lupande Game Management Areas and South Luangwa National Park**

Asia

10. **Indonesia, Dumoga-Bone National Park**
11. **Indonesia, Gunung Leuser National Park**
12. **Nepal, Annapurna Conservation Area**
13. **Nepal, Royal Chitwan National Park**
14. **Thailand, Khao Yai National Park**

Latin America

15. **Costa Rica, Osa Peninsula**
16. **Costa Rica, Talamanca Region**
17. **Mexico, Monarch Butterfly Overwintering Reserves**
18. **Mexico, Sian Ka'an Biosphere Reserve**
19. **Peru, Central Selva**

Box 1.1 Case study protected areas: sites and projects
(See appendix for more information; all dollar amounts are current U.S. dollars.)

Africa

Air-Tenere National Nature Reserve, Niger. This 77,000 square kilometer game reserve was established in 1988. A 1982–86 conservation project was the forerunner to a three-year $2.5 million project emphasizing conservation, protection, and rural development in and adjacent to the reserve. The earlier project was funded by the World Wildlife Fund International, IUCN, and the government of Niger.

Amboseli National Park, Kenya. A 1977 World Bank loan supported tourism development, water-point development, and community services to compensate local people for loss of access to the 600 square kilometer park. The separate, community-based Wildlife Extension project, which aims to improve local participation and use of wildlife, has an annual budget of $50,000.

Beza Mahafaly and Andohahela Reserves, Madagascar. One Malagasy and two American universities helped local people establish the 6 square kilometer Beza reserve in 1985. The project has implemented local development and conservation programs and recently was expanded to include the 760 square kilometer Andohahela. Funding for 1977–89 was $450,000.

Bururi Forest Reserve, Burundi. The Bururi project promotes conservation and forestry activities around a 20 square kilometer forest reserve, begun with USAID funding of $1.2 million from 1983–87. Replication is under way at three other reserves, totaling 58 square kilometers, with funding of $500,000 for 1986–91.

East Usambara Mountains Forest Reserves, Tanzania. This patchwork of eighteen forest reserves covering 16 square kilometers has been threatened by logging and shifting cultivation. A government project with technical assistance from IUCN has worked in fifteen villages to promote conservation and development since 1987. Funding for 1987–91 was $1.5 million.

Nazinga Game Ranch, Burkina Faso. A 940 square kilometer ranch was established to protect dwindling wildlife and provide local communities with benefits from employment, safari hunting, tourism, and meat production. Government and Canadian International Development Agency funding was $3.1 million during 1979–89.

South Luangwa National Park, Zambia. This is a 9,050 square kilometer park surrounded by game management areas. The Lupande project, replicated as the national Administrative Design for Game Management Areas (ADMADE) program, promotes return of safari hunting revenues to local communities, job creation, and antipoaching in a game management area. Annual funds are $50,000 for the pilot project and $3 million over four years for the ADMADE project. The Luangwa Integrated Rural Development project (LIRDP), initiated in 1988, is a large, regional project with funding of $25 million for five years. Both projects are being implemented by the government of Zambia.

Volcanoes National Park, Rwanda. The 150 square kilometer park is surrounded by intensive agriculture. Since 1979, an African Wildlife Foundation project has attempted to protect the park's gorillas and promote tourism. Funding exceeds $250,000 annually.

Asia

Annapurna Conservation Area, Nepal. This 2,600 square kilometer multiple-use area was established in 1986 under the jurisdiction of Nepal's leading nongovernmental organization, the King Mahendra Trust for Nature Conservation, to mitigate the effects of tourism on the environment and to promote local development. The 1986–89 cost was $450,000; total project revenues from all sources from 1989 to 1991 are about $200,000 a year.

Dumoga-Bone National Park, Indonesia. The 3,000 square kilometer park was established in 1982 to protect the rivers supplying two irrigation projects used by 8,000 farmers to grow paddy rice. Funding was provided by a $60 million World Bank loan, about $1 million of which was used to establish the park.

Gunung Leuser National Park, Indonesia. The 9,000 square kilometer park is acutely threatened by agricultural encroachment and logging, both facilitated by road construction. Buffer zones have been delineated but not implemented.

Khao Yai National Park, Thailand. The 2,200 square kilometer park, an important tourist attraction, is threatened by logging, poaching, and the development of incompatible tourist facilities. Two Thai nongovernmental organizations began a project in one of 150 villages on the park border in 1985 to promote conservation through development, later expanding into several other communities. The 1985–89 cost was $500,000.

Royal Chitwan National Park, Nepal. The 900 square kilometer park, established in 1973, is a premier tourist attraction surrounded by a rapidly growing population. Park officials permit villagers to collect grasses once a year for house construction and thatching.

Latin America

Central Selva, Peru. This is the site of the 1,220 square kilometer Yanachanga-Chemillen National Park and forest and indigenous reserves. A $22 million USAID-funded project (1982–87) was initiated to maximize sustained productivity of the watershed and increase local income. From 1988 to the present the World Wildlife Fund-U.S. has provided $100,000 in support for the Yanesha Forestry Cooperative, implemented by the Amuesha Indians once USAID support ended.

Monarch Butterfly Overwintering Reserves, Mexico. A cluster of five mountaintop reserves, totaling 5 square kilometers, protects butterflies. A Mexican nongovernmental organization is working to promote tourism and educa-

Box 1.1 cont.

tion in local communities and reduce the high level of illegal logging that threatens the tiny reserves. The World Wildlife Fund contributed more than $250,000 in 1985–90.

Osa Peninsula, Costa Rica. The 1,750 square kilometer peninsula includes several protected areas, all threatened by logging. The Boscosa projec,t initiated in 1987 by the World Wildlife Fund, supports income-generating activities and local organizational activities. Funding from various sources for the Boscosa project has been approximately $850,000 for 1988–91.

Sian Ka'an Biosphere Reserve, Mexico. This 5,200-square-kilometer multiple-use reserve includes terrestrial and marine habitats. A local nongovernmental organization, Amigos de Sian Ka'an, supports the reserve and its residents through small-scale development and publicity, with less than $100,000 annually. The nearby Pilot Forestry Plan also works with local communities on their collective landholdings to improve forestry practices.

Talamanca Region, Costa Rica. The region includes a variety of protected areas, including the Gandoca-Manzanillo Wildlife Refuge. A Costa Rican nongovernmental organization has promoted small-scale development activities emphasizing sustainable development practices in the region since the early 1980s. Funding was $1.2 million in 1984–88 from numerous donors.

2. Protected areas and their neighbors

This chapter describes the variety in site conditions facing project managers as they began their work and discusses the implications of these conditions for project design, implementation, and effectiveness. The initial site conditions can be characterized in terms of the physical and ecological attributes of the protected area, the institutional arrangements for its management, and the political, cultural, and socioeconomic characteristics of the surrounding communities—including any constraints imposed by the presence of the protected area. In some cases the local human dynamics were as intricate as the biological systems the project were working to conserve.

Understanding the complex and variable relationships between the protected areas and their local communities—particularly any threats to the protected area posed by local people's activities—requires site-specific analysis. We therefore explored the extent to which the design and implementation of integrated conservation-development projects (ICDPs) appeared to be based on an appropriate level of understanding of local site conditions.

Protected areas and surrounding lands

The most obvious feature of the protected areas represented in our case studies is their wide variation in size, from Niger's 65,000 square kilometer Air-Tenere National Nature Reserve in the southern Sahara to the 5 square kilometer Monarch Butterfly Overwintering Reserves in Mexico (table 2.1).

Not surprisingly, there is no clear relationship between the size of a protected area and the necessary scale of an ICDP. The nature, extent, and distribution of local human activity, as well as local people-park relations, are as important for ICDP design and implementation as the absolute size of the protected area (ICDP scale issues are discussed in more detail in chapter 8).

In addition to size, the case study parks and surrounding lands vary dramatically in physical and ecological characteristics—from wet to dry, flat to mountainous, fertile to barren—and in the degree of transformation experienced as a result of human activity. They also contain different sets of plants and animals. There appeared to be few generalizable implications, except that—because most ICDPs were in rural areas—the best opportunities for ICDP-generated income gains occurred where conditions were favorable for agriculture—wet climate and flat, fertile land. (Conditions at specific sites are described in the appendix, and some project activities designed to take advantage of local conditions are discussed in chapter 5.)

The case study protected areas can be divided into traditional parks and multiple-use areas. Following the classifications of the International Union for Conservation of Nature and Natural Resources (IUCN), the traditional parks largely correspond to category II, national parks, but include categories I and III (see table 1.1 in chapter 1). The multiple-use areas largely correspond to category VIII, multiple-use management areas and managed resource areas, but also include categories V and VII. Biosphere reserves—which were not classified—are a type of multiple-use area.

Traditional parks

Traditional parks totally excluded local people from consideration when they were initially established. Parks in this category include Andohahela (Madagascar), Bururi and Rumonge (Burundi), Chitwan (Nepal), Corcovado (Costa Rica), Gunung Leuser (Indonesia), Khao Yai (Thailand), Luangwa (Zambia), Usambara (Tanzania), Volcanoes (Rwanda), and Yanachanga-Chemillen (Peru). Management of these parks has been oriented toward enforcement and has been generally unsympathetic to the needs of the local population. People who had been living inside the parks were either forcibly evicted or allowed to remain in small enclaves inside the boundaries but legally excluded from the parks.

Table 2.1 Case study protected areas

Region/country	Protected area	Size (sq km)	Project
Africa			
Burkina Faso	Nazinga Game Ranch	940	Nazinga Game Ranch
Burundi	Bururi Forest Reserve	20	Bururi Forest project
	Rumonge, Vyanda, and Kigwena Reserves	58	Rumonge Agroforestry project
Kenya	Amboseli National Park	488	Amboseli Park Agreement Wildlife Extension project
Madagascar	Andohahela Integral Reserve	760	Conservation in Southern Madagascar project
	Beza Mahafaly Special Reserve Area	6	Conservation in Southern Madagascar project
Niger	Air-Tenere Nature Reserve	65,000	Air-Tenere Conservation and Management of Natural Resources project
Rwanda	Volcanoes National Park	150	Mountain Gorilla project
Tanzania	East Usambara Mountains	160	East Usambara Agricultural Development and Environmental Conservation project
Zambia	Lupande Game Management Areas	4,840	Lupande Development project
	South Luangwa National Park	9,050	Administrative Design for Game Management Areas program (ADMADE) Luangwa Integrated Rural Development Project (LIRDP)
Asia			
Indonesia	Dumoga-Bone National Park	3,000	Kosinggolan and Toraut irrigation projects
	Gunung Leuser National Park	9,000	None
Nepal	Annapurna Conservation Area	2,600	Annapurna Conservation Area project
	Royal Chitwan National Park	900	Village Grass Collection
Thailand	Khao Yai National Park	2,200	Sup Tai Rural Development for Conservation project and the Environmental Awareness and Development Mobilization (TEAM) project
Latin America			
Costa Rica	Osa Peninsula		Boscosa project
	Corcovado National Park	400	
	Golfo Dulce Forest Reserve		
	Guaymi Indigenous Reserve		
	Isla de Cano Biological Reserve		
	Golfito Forest Reserve		
	Talamanca Region		ANAI Talamanca project
	Gandoca-Manzanillo Wildlife refuge	50	
	La Amistad Biosphere Reserve	2,000	
Mexico	Monarch Butterfly Overwintering Reserves	5	Monarch Butterfly Overwintering Reserve Protection
	Sian Ka'an Biosphere Reserve	5,230	Amigos de Sian Ka'an (ASK) Community Development project Pilot Forestry Management and Processing Plan (PFP)
Peru	Central Selva		Central Selva Resource Management project
	San Matias-San Carlos Protection Forest	1,500	
	Yanachanga-Chemillen National Park	1,220	
	Yanesha Communal Reserve	350	Yanesha Communal Forestry project

Source: Compiled by authors, based on site visits.

These parks were already well-established before the projects began, and local people-park relations were invariably already poor, if not hostile (box 2.1). All of these parks were under considerable pressure from local human activities, and several had already become seriously degraded before the projects began.

Management plans exist for most of the traditional parks included in the study. Many were prepared when the parks were established, with foreign funding and technical assistance. Some of the more recent plans recommend considering local perspectives as a part of park management, but little explicit guidance is provided on how this might be done. Few of these recommendations have been implemented, largely because of funding shortages.

The authority of traditional park management usually does not extend beyond park boundaries or into human enclaves in the park. Legal jurisdiction over the lands and people adjacent to the park is usually shared by other agencies of the national government and the local governments. Thus traditional park management agencies rarely can legally initiate an ICDP outside a traditional park, even if they want to and have the funding.

Some of the traditional protected areas are bordered or surrounded by forested areas that have been designated for timber production or watershed protection, and where permanent settlement is illegal, as in Indonesia and Thailand. Some of the ICDPs in this study were directed toward communities occupying these restricted areas. In Thailand, for example, several million people live and farm illegally in national forest reserves. Many of the Thai national parks are bordered by villages occupying these reserves. Government agencies are frequently unable or unwilling to support, or even to condone, development activities directed toward these illegal settlements, considerably complicating any attempt to launch ICDP initiatives.

In some cases, people will be willing to be resettled from traditional parks if they receive compensation (see Osa Peninsula case, box 2.1). In other cases, resettlement is involuntary and can lead to conflict, especially when people feel that their traditional lands have been usurped to create a park or reserve. (See Cernea 1988a for a discussion of resettlement in World Bank-financed projects.)

The case study projects linked to traditional parks have all been directed toward villages just outside the park boundaries. The projects were implemented by organizations that were administratively distinct from the park managers. Relationships between the project and park managers have proved to be key factors determining a project's effectiveness. (For more detail, see chapter 7.)

Multiple-use areas

The multiple-use area case studies can be divided in two groups. First are protected areas that specifically permit human settlement and natural resource use, within designated zones, inside a larger multiple-use area that also includes fully protected zones. These include the case study sites at Air-Tenere (Niger), Annapurna (Nepal), Sian Ka'an (Mexico), and the game management areas around

---

Box 2.1 People-park conflicts

Gunung Leuser, Indonesia. Local resentment of the park is particularly strong in Aceh Tenggara District, where 82 percent of the land has been set aside for conservation. The underequipped and understaffed national park guards appear to have had no effect on the rapid forest destruction resulting from illegal logging and agricultural encroachment. Park officials who reported illegal practices to the police or local government authorities have been threatened. Any new initiatives would appear doomed without a fundamental shift in the relationship between the park managers, the local government, and village communities.

Khao Yai, Thailand. Enforcement measures following the establishment of the national park met with hostility and resulted in armed clashes between Royal Forestry Department personnel and villagers, with loss of life on both sides. Despite aggressive protection measures, illegal activities in the park have continued, mainly poaching and the removal of timber and other forest products. In the first four months of 1986, for example, 258 poachers were arrested in the park. By the mid-1980s, at least 5 percent of the park's forests had been lost to encroachment and perhaps another 5 to 10 percent degraded.

Osa Peninsula, Costa Rica. Displaced workers from abandoned banana plantations invaded Corcovado National Park on the Osa Peninsula in 1985. The government was unable to stop the invasion, and hundreds of people began panning for gold, a process that causes severe damage to rivers through sedimentation and mercury pollution. A court order forced the police to evict the miners, after compensatory benefits were negotiated between the outgoing government and the nearly eight hundred miners and their families. New squatters soon invaded the park and attempts to evict them have escalated to armed conflicts.

Luangwa (Zambia). Second are traditional parks that expressly provide for local social and economic development outside the park boundaries. These parks and reserves were established at the same time or after the beginning of the ICDP: Beza Mahafaly (Madagascar), Amboseli (Kenya), and Dumoga-Bone (Indonesia). Although a few countries have passed legislation that establishes or permits multiple-use conservation areas (box 2.2), establishing them in most countries would require new legislation.

Multiple-use areas have two advantages over traditional parks for implementing ICDPS. First, the multiple-use area legislation generally establishes a single management authority responsible for both the fully protected zones—where no hunting, farming, or other human use is permitted—and the zones set aside for human use. Granting such sole jurisdiction can simplify ICDP management and facilitate coordination of a project's development and conservation components.

The second advantage derives from the fact that the multiple-use approach is, by definition, more supportive of local communities. Not surprisingly, it has proved easier for ICDPs to establish positive relations with local people who feel their aspirations, needs, and opinions have been taken into account—regardless of whether they support the conservation objectives of the fully protected zones. ICDPs at multiple-use areas rarely have to deal with the entrenched resentment and hostility that can build up outside the borders of a traditional park.

Simply put, an ICDP consists of *conservation* activities, in parks or in the fully protected zones of multiple-use areas, and *development* activities, outside traditional parks or inside the human-use zones of multiple-use areas. At a traditional park site, ICDP development activities based on positive incentives are usually attempting to modify a history of punitive, enforcement-oriented park management. At multiple-use areas, however, there are far greater opportunities to balance—and establish linkages between—development and conservation.

Local threats to protected areas

What are threats? They have been defined as "activities of human or natural origin that cause significant damage to park resources, or are in serious conflict with the objectives of park administration and management" (Machlis and Tichnell 1985, 13). Local threats to protected areas in developing countries usually arise from unsustainable exploitation through hunting, agricultural encroachment, burning, logging, the collection of forest products, or a combination of these. However, this partial list provides little insight into the underlying factors motivating the people carrying out these activities, or how they might be induced to modify them. These underlying factors can vary dramatically from one protected area to another or even within a single protected area.

It is extremely difficult to generalize about threats to protected areas in any useful way. The

---

Box 2.2 Innovative legislation for multiple-use conservation areas

Air-Tenere, Niger. Legislation originally permitted three types of protected areas in Niger: total game reserves, with access generally limited to researchers; partial game reserves, allowing hunting of certain species; and national parks, where exploitation is forbidden but tourism is allowed. Legislation passed in 1988 provided legal support for a conservation project in the Air-Tenere region (under way since 1982), establishing a total game reserve (the Addax Sanctuary) of 12,805 square kilometers within a partial game reserve of 77,360 square kilometers. The Addax Sanctuary was established in unused areas. The remainder, the Air-Tenere National Nature Reserve, was designed to promote the continued use of natural resources by the indigenous population. Resident populations were assured of the rights to settle, move freely throughout the reserve, and collect dead wood, medicinal plants, and so on; however, hunting and "needless" damage of vegetation are forbidden.

Annapurna, Nepal. In 1985, the King of Nepal issued a directive to manage tourism while safeguarding the environment in the highly stressed Annapurna region. Surveys of local residents found resistance to a national park designation, similar to opposition elsewhere in Nepal where national parks have been associated with resettlements and a significant Army presence. A "Conservation Area" was recommended. In contrast to national parks, conservation areas are each divided into zones, some of which allow hunting, collection of forest products, allocation of visitor fees for local development, and delegation of management authority to the village level. Legislation was passed in 1986 to establish the Annapurna Conservation Area and initiate the Annapurna Conservation Area project.

Game Management Areas, Zambia. Two legislative changes lie behind the Lupande and Luangwa projects. The first change, extended to numerous governmental agencies, was the authority to establish revolving funds. This allowed different agencies, in this case the National Parks and Wildlife Service, control over revenues, which in turn enabled them to share hunting fees with local communities. A second change permitted government agencies to hire non-civil servants. This created a flexible hiring system allowing the National Parks and Wildlife Service complete control in establishing the Village Scout Program, which employs local people as wildlife scouts.

few studies that have attempted to compare types of threats have generally been unsatisfactory and have concentrated on the visible manifestations instead of the underlying causes (box 2.3). These studies do not adequately distinguish causes and symptoms (for example, "local attitudes" or "human encroachment"), give little insight into the causes of particular threats, and do not identify the relative significance of the threats.

One reason for the difficulty in analyzing even site-specific threats is that many of their fundamental causes lie well beyond protected area boundaries. For example, illegal timber cutting inside parks could have multiple causes, including migration into regions with undeveloped labor markets, changing agricultural practices, high population growth, new access to forest product markets, government pricing policies, the need to convert savings to cash, and so on. Different groups—whether based on ethnic origin, social class, or other characteristics—may respond differently to any of these changes. Such levels of complexity were common among the communities targeted by the case study projects.

The most evident *proximate* threats to the case study protected areas are shown in box 2.4, although these descriptions do not present the underlying causes. (These are described, where known, in the appendix.) Rapid population growth—through natural increase or migration—

is one of the most pervasive threats to protected areas worldwide, including many of the case study sites. The threats to at least four of the sites are partly attributable to the collapse of formerly dominant natural resource industries. The demise of banana production near the Osa Peninsula and of cacao at Talamanca, both in Costa Rica; coffee and then tea in Tanzania's Usambara mountains; and mahogany at Sian Ka'an, Mexico, all led to substantial local changes. With the loss of jobs and the lack of alternative employment in these regions, people stepped up the rate of conversion of forested land to agriculture and intensified logging for timber.

The activities of local people may well represent the most immediate, direct, and visible threat. But in many cases the rising pressures on natural ecosystems derive from laws, policies, social changes, and economic forces over which poor rural people have no influence yet which can severely curtail their options. This suggests that serious efforts to conserve biodiversity must extend beyond local communities.

The areas surrounding parks and other protected areas have generally been portrayed as marginal for agriculture, remote from markets and employment opportunities, and lacking services, roads, and infrastructure, and the people as poor, with little political influence. While the case study sites reveal a measure of truth in such characterizations, they are simplistic. The communities ad-

---

Box 2.3 Studies of threats to protected areas

In the early 1980s a study by the IUCN (1984) summarized the kinds of threats facing forty-three of the world's most threatened protected areas. The top ten reported threats were
1. Inadequate management resources
2. Human encroachment
3. Change in water regime or hydro development
4. Poaching
5. Adjacent land development
6. Inappropriate internal development (for example, roads)
7. Mining and prospecting
8. Livestock conflicts
9. Military activity
10. Forestry activities.
A subsequent survey of 135 parks in more than 50 countries (Machlis and Tichnell 1985) reported the most common threats as
1. Illegal removal of animal life
2. Lack of management personnel
3. Removal of vegetation
4. Soil erosion
5. Local attitudes
6. Conflicting demands on management
7. Fire
8. Human harassment of animals
9. Loss of habitat
10. Vegetation trampling.

Box 2.4 Proximate threats to protected areas

Africa

Air-Tenere, Niger	Tourism, poaching, livestock grazing during droughts
Amboseli, Kenya	Livestock grazing, tourism
Bururi/Rumonge, Burundi	Fuelwood collection, grazing, agricultural encroachment, fire
East Usambara, Tanzania	Agricultural encroachment, logging
Beza Mahafaly, Madagascar	Livestock grazing
Andohahela, Madagascar	Poaching, agricultural encroachment, burning
Luangwa, Zambia	Poaching
Nazinga, Burkina Faso	Poaching
Volcanoes, Rwanda	Hunting, agricultural encroachment

Asia

Annapurna, Nepal	Fuelwood collection, water pollution, poor sanitation, littering
Dumoga-Bone, Indonesia	Poaching, agricultural encroachment
Gunung-Leuser, Indonesia	Road construction, logging, agricultural encroachment
Khao Yai, Thailand	Agriculture, poaching, logging, inappropriate development
Chitwan, Nepal	Fuelwood collection, livestock grazing

Latin America

Monarch, Mexico	Logging, agriculture, cattle grazing
Osa, Costa Rica	Logging, gold-mining, agricultural expansion
Central Selva, Peru	Colonization, agricultural expansion, cattle-ranching
Sian Ka'an, Mexico	Logging
Talamanca, Costa Rica	Road construction, agricultural expansion, tourism

---

jacent to these protected areas are not homogenous. They vary considerably in their social and political systems, economic activities, institutions and authority structures, history and longevity at particular sites, and linkages with regional, national, and international economies (box 2.5). Variations in these characteristics *within* areas are in some cases as significant as variations *between* different areas. Understanding the interaction of these variables helps in understanding the local threats facing the case study protected areas.

Information gathering

Comparison of the case study sites has emphasized the difficulty in generalizing about the extent to which local communities pose an ultimate, proximate, direct, or indirect threat—or no threat—to parks; this is a site-specific judgment. Thus ICDP design should be based on detailed site-specific studies of the local socioeconomic, political, and cultural contexts.

A few of the case study projects conducted particularly effective surveys. In Nepal, a three-member survey team spent six months collecting information on what became the multiple-use Annapurna Conservation Area, developing a provisional management plan based on discussions with community leaders and villagers throughout the region. At Khao Yai, interviews with Sup Tai villagers conducted by the Population and Community Development Association of Thailand, a nongovernmental organization, revealed how extensive a stranglehold local moneylenders had on the local economy. In Costa Rica, the Boscosa project carried out socioeconomic surveys, land-use studies, and forest inventories, which were used to initiate planning with the local community and to provide baseline data for the project. The process of collecting this information provided an important opening to effective local participation in these three projects. Among the remaining projects, Amboseli (Kenya), Lupande (Zambia), and Nazinga (Burkina Faso) were originated by people who knew the areas and their communities intimately. Other ICDPs started with much less information.

Several techniques for gathering advance knowledge about communities are available (see, for example, Carruthers and Chambers 1981, CIDE and NES 1990, Gregersen 1988, Kumar 1987, Molnar 1989, and Noronha 1980). However, except for those described above, the case study projects did not conduct socioeconomic assessments of their targeted beneficiaries—either because they did not recognize the importance of gathering systematic information on local people or had inadequate resources. Most projects thus began with a very limited understanding of the dynamics underlying the threats to the protected areas they were seeking to protect.

Box 2.5 Variations in community characteristics of communities in or around protected areas

Ethnicity. In some areas, local populations are ethnically heterogeneous (Annapurna, Nepal; Usambara, Tanzania); in some there are several prevalent groups (Dumoga-Bone, Indonesia; Khao Yai, Thailand; Talamanca, Costa Rica; Volcanoes, Rwanda); and in some, populations are relatively homogeneous (Air-Tenere, Niger; Amboseli, Kenya; Beza Mahafaly, Madagascar; Corcovado, Costa Rica).

Numbers. Population densities range from very high (Bururi, Burundi; Chitwan, Nepal; Dumoga-Bone, Indonesia; Monarch, Mexico; Volcanoes, Rwanda) to very low (Air-Tenere, Niger; Amboseli, Kenya; Annapurna, Nepal; Lupande/ADMADE, Zambia; Sian Ka'an, Mexico).

Length of residence. Some communities are well-established (Air-Tenere, Niger; Amboseli, Kenya; Annapurna, Nepal; Beza Mahafaly, Madagascar; Lupande/ADMADE, Zambia), while others consist of recent migrants (Chitwan, Nepal; Dumoga-Bone, Indonesia; Monarch, Mexico; Osa, Costa Rica; Usambara, Tanzania). In other areas, long-standing populations, often indigenous groups, faced a rapid influx of migrants (Central Selva, Peru; Sian Ka'an, Mexico; Talamanca, Costa Rica).

Local organizations. Responsibility for decisionmaking rested with elected officials (Beza Mahafaly, Madagascar; Monarch, Mexico), government appointees (Nazinga, Burkina Faso; Usambara, Tanzania), traditional leaders (Air-Tenere, Niger; Amboseli, Kenya; Lupande/ADMADE, Zambia) and combinations of these. Some communities appeared to lack organized decisionmaking mechanisms (chapter 6).

Location and access. Most sites are remote from cities and markets, although recent road construction has made some areas accessible (Dumoga-Bone and Gunung Leuser, Indonesia; Khao Yai, Thailand; Talamanca, Costa Rica) (chapter 5).

Tourism. Some areas draw substantial numbers of tourists (Air-Tenere, Niger; Amboseli, Kenya; Annapurna and Chitwan, Nepal; Monarch, Mexico; Volcanoes, Rwanda). More government services tend to be provided in such areas, although services are usually oriented toward tourists, not local communities (chapter 5).

Land and resource use. Most areas were heavily dependent on the land and the natural resource base for subsistence. Predominant use patterns were pastoralism (Amboseli, Kenya); agriculture (Dumoga-Bone, Indonesia; Lupande/ADMADE, Zambia); mixed agriculture and pastoralism (Air-Tenere, Niger; Andohahela and Beza Mahafaly, Madagascar); and mixed agriculture and forestry (Beza Mahafaly, Madagascar; Bururi and Rumonge, Burundi; Monarch and Sian Ka'an, Mexico; Osa and Talamanca, Costa Rica; Usambara, Tanzania; Volcanoes, Rwanda). These ranged from traditional systems for subsistence production (Amboseli, Kenya; Central Selva, Peru) to subsistence and commercial sectors in the same area (Osa and Talamanca, Costa Rica) (chapter 5).

3. Case study projects in Costa Rica, Tanzania, and Thailand

The previous chapter described how the case study projects faced a wide variety of local conditions when their work began. These variations added to the complexity of an already challenging task—to reconcile local people to a new or established protected area. In this chapter the focus shifts to the projects.

The approaches to project design and implementation varied; and no single project was typical. It is therefore very difficult to characterize integrated conservation-development projects (ICDPs) with a tidy definition. Assessments of the projects for this study were strongly influenced by an appreciation of the subtleties in local context, many of which became apparent only from site visits and interviews with project staff and members of the local communities who were expected to benefit from the projects. Some of these subtleties disappeared again when the case study analyses were condensed for the appendix. So, case study projects in three protected areas are given more thorough treatment here: the Talamanca region in Costa Rica, the East Usambara mountains in Tanzania, and Khao Yai in Thailand. Although the choice of these examples was subjective, they illustrate issues and lessons applicable to many of the case studies.

Talamanca Region, Costa Rica

Context

Talamanca county is in the extreme southeastern section of Costa Rica, bordered on the east by the Caribbean Sea and on the south by Panama (see map 3.1). Ecosystems in the project area include beaches, coral reefs, coastal plains, fresh water swamps and mangroves, tropical moist forest, and an inland mountain area that rises to nearly 4,000 meters. Talamanca has two national parks, one biological reserve, one protected zone, five indigenous reservations, and a wildlife refuge; along with other lands, these comprise part of La Amistad Biosphere Reserve, which extends through much of the county. A variety of endangered species live in the protected areas in the region.

Commercial banana production is prevalent in the flat areas bordering the Sixaola river. Smallholder agriculture, mainly plantain and root crop production for export, predominates in the rest of the Sixaola floodplain. Elsewhere, cacao was the principal source of income for many small farmers until 1980, when monilia pod rot, a fungal disease, devastated production in the region. The Talamanca region is one of the most racially heterogeneous zones in the country, with three primary ethnic groups: blacks, mestizos (mixed Spaniards and Indians), and Indians.

Despite a long history of plantation agriculture in the region, many of the hillsides are heavily forested, although many of the trees are secondary growth. Cacao and coconut production and fishing were the major economic activities along the coast, but they have been replaced by tourism, land speculation, and logging. The rapidly eroding beaches near Puerto Viejo are becoming increasingly popular for surfing, fishing, tourism, and other recreational uses.

In the last ten years the Costa Rican government has built numerous roads throughout the region. Tourism grew and land prices increased rapidly once the travel time from the Central Valley to the Talamancan coast was shortened. But the road building has also resulted in deforestation along the new roads. Timber contractors seeking lumber and migrants looking for agricultural land have been clearing the forest where roads have provided access. One reason for the migrants' actions is that Costa Rican law requires land improvements to establish property rights. The result has been that new migrants cleared land to claim it and old-time farmers suddenly cleared land to stop migrants from claiming their land—resulting in high levels of deforestation.

Map 3.1 Talamanca Region, Costa Rica

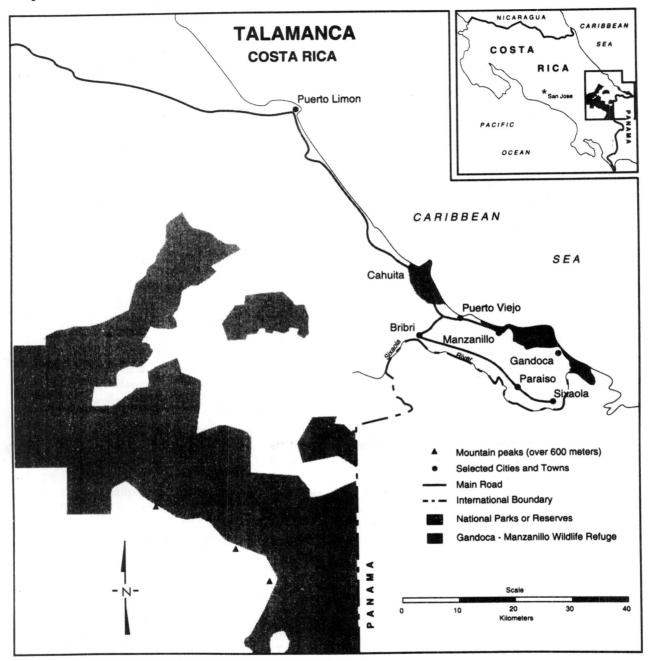

Project

ANAI is a Costa Rican nongovernmental organization that has worked in Talamanca since 1976 to integrate conservation of natural ecosystems with the development needs of rural peoples. The Development Research Corporation for the Socio-Environment (CIDESA), founded by one of ANAI's staff, works closely with ANAI on this project, especially on issues related to community participation. ANAI's principal objective, according to project papers, is to promote individual responsibility for land stewardship, based on the belief that "the most apt stewards of tropical lands are the peasants who have committed their lives to them. Whatever aids these peoples helps the tropical environment and vice versa." ANAI has initiated or supported a variety of activities throughout the region.

With funding from World Wildlife Fund-U.S., ANAI began a land titling project in connection with proposals to establish the Gandoca-Manzanillo wildlife refuge. The 50 square kilometers proposed for reserve status consisted of private and unclaimed lands, some under cultivation and some wild. This activity involved creating a new category of protected area that would allow private ownership subject to restrictions on use. When ANAI heard that a road was to be constructed through the proposed refuge, it asked the government to officially decree the refuge as soon as possible. This partially undermined the process of community dialogue that ANAI had initiated. ANAI not only promoted establishment of the refuge, but has played an important role in emphasizing its protection. ANAI financed protection activities until the Costa Rican government took over responsibility in 1989.

ANAI helped farmers occupying land in or next to the refuge with the complicated titling process. Bureaucratic snags have turned what was to have been a quick process into a five-year effort. Two communities have bought farmland on which they intend to retain forest on 70 percent of the land. Another community near the refuge has accepted land-use restrictions.

ANAI has also been active in protecting the four species of marine sea turtles that nest on the beaches and has initiated research on lobster and butterflies. Field trials with ornamental and medicinal plants are under way to test their adaptability to the agroecology of Talamanca. With the assistance of the Green Iguana Foundation, ANAI has also started two projects to raise green iguana. The program is intended to provide local residents with a source of protein and income, relieve pressure on wild iguanas, and justify maintaining the forest cover.

ANAI has helped forty communities in Talamanca establish nurseries, with nearly 600 smallholder farmers participating. The nurseries emphasize stabilizing incomes through crop diversification, promoting reforestation, improving soil management, and promoting environmental education and community organization. ANAI promotes the planting of tree crops that can absorb surplus labor, unlike slash-and-burn agriculture, and that will provide a stable and diversified production base for local communities. Cacao has been the most popular species. ANAI estimates that since the inception of the project, more than 1.8 million cacao trees have been distributed throughout the area.

ANAI has two experimental farms, with 80 hectares of tropical plants and 120 hectares of forest, that it uses to test for new agroforestry and agricultural species. CIDESA has also initiated a small-scale organic farming plot in one of the local communities, and a women's vegetable gardening project. In 1989, ANAI began the community technicians program to develop local leaders who can provide information for agricultural and agroforestry development and can act as liaisons between their community and outside agencies. ANAI also helped create a regional procurement, processing, and marketing association.

Other activities include environmental education and training, support to communities on tourism development, and work with the Indian groups on oral histories and other activities.

Evaluation and lessons

- ANAI has been active in the Talamanca region for more than ten years. Its activities are not an integrated program but a collection of small-scale rural development activities widely spread throughout the region.
- The national government has supported ANAI's efforts financially and politically. The head of the National Park Service commented that ANAI and CIDESA have influenced the government's perception of the importance of promoting development activities with protected area management. This may have an important influence on Costa Rica's evolving park management structure.
- Relations between ANAI and the municipality of Talamanca have been strained. The municipality would like to attract large-scale development and feels that potentially large tax revenues have already been lost because of the conservation-oriented use restrictions promoted by ANAI. The municipality sees conservation as thwarting local economic development, instead of supporting it.
- External factors, such as road building and government delays in granting land title, have influenced local perceptions of ANAI. Although the refuge is protected, misunderstandings and uneven local support continue to be problems—eroding local confidence in ANAI and making the organization the target of frequent rumors. And the refuge designation has not deterred development.
- The communities actively participate in nursery management and other project activities. There is also some limited, informal participation in design and evaluation of some project components. But there is no formal emphasis on building local

institutions, although ANAI is strengthening local leadership ability through the community technicians and nursery programs.

• The community nursery program—the most visible and well-established program component—has succeeded in terms of community participation in decisionmaking, the number of communities involved, and the number of seedlings produced. But the greatest number of seedlings have been cacao plants, which could cause problems if prices continue to fall. This problem highlights the difficulty of balancing decisionmaking with sound technical decisions: ANAI staff view themselves as technical specialists who can provide the farmers with guidance, but they are unwilling to dictate what should be planted—and they note that the farmers are most interested in producing cacao seedlings.

• Despite the project's experimental nature, ANAI documented little of the activities, obstacles, key issues, or ways to replicate the project. It will be difficult for ANAI or other organizations to assess which activities were successful and why.

• Although many of the development activities have a conservation orientation, ANAI's conservation and development activities have no explicit linkage. Its activities do not focus on any specific protected area in the Talamanca region, although its role in the formation of the Gandoca-Manzanillo Wildlife Refuge was vital and its interest in protecting La Amistad Biosphere Reserve is strong. The difficulty in establishing direct linkages in areas undergoing rapid change was evident in a 1987 external evaluation of the project:

Thus far ANAI has concentrated its effort on immediate issues: agroforestry technology, appropriate roads, creation of the refuge, and land titling. Several of these issues have been resolved satisfactorily and the others appear headed for satisfactory resolution. Even if all are resolved, however, ANAI will not have fully attained its dual goals of development and conservation. In particular the conservation goal will remain in jeopardy because population will increase; lands will be sold to new farmers; existing farmers will intensify land use and also bring more land into production; forests and wildlife products will increase in value. (McCaffrey and Landazuri 1987, 32)

• Lack of secure long-term funding has prevented ANAI from increasing project activities and making long-term project commitments. This also has meant that much of the director's time is spent fund-raising and reporting.

East Usambara Mountains, Tanzania

Context

Located in northeastern Tanzania, the East Usambara mountains cover about 32,000 hectares with a high point of 1,500 meters (see map 3.2). The mountains belong to the Eastern Arc, a comparatively old and isolated mountain chain with a remarkably high degree of biological endemism. The mountains contain high-quality hardwood forests and are the principal source of water for streams that supply urban and agricultural areas in the surrounding lowlands.

Once extensive forests have been replaced by a patchwork of shrinking forest remnants, many of them modified by human activity, mainly tea estates and smallholder farms. The forest remnants include eighteen forest reserves covering about 160 square kilometers and 90 square kilometers of public land that has not been cleared for agriculture. Industrial logging (until 1987) and cardamom cultivation have significantly degraded the area's natural forests.

The forest reserves are under the jurisdiction of the Forestry and Beekeeping Division of the Ministry of Lands, Natural Resources, and Tourism. District authorities have jurisdiction over the public lands and the estates. Local people also have considerable—but unclear—rights over the public lands.

The East Usambara population of about 40,000 consists almost entirely of poor farmers from several ethnic groups. Many are migrants to the area, attracted by wage labor opportunities in private coffee and tea estates. Tea and cardamom are now the principal crops. Cardamom is a major export crop for Tanzania, and production has been encouraged by the government. Cardamom cultivation requires shade, which the natural forest canopy provides, but it degrades the soil after a few years of production, requiring the clearing of more plots. Since industrial logging ended in 1987 in response to international pressure, cardamom cultivation has been the greatest single threat to the remaining forests.

Project

The East Usambara Agricultural Development and Environmental Conservation project began in early 1987; according to project papers, its goals were "improving the villagers' living conditions and

Map 3.2 East Usambara Mountains, Tanzania

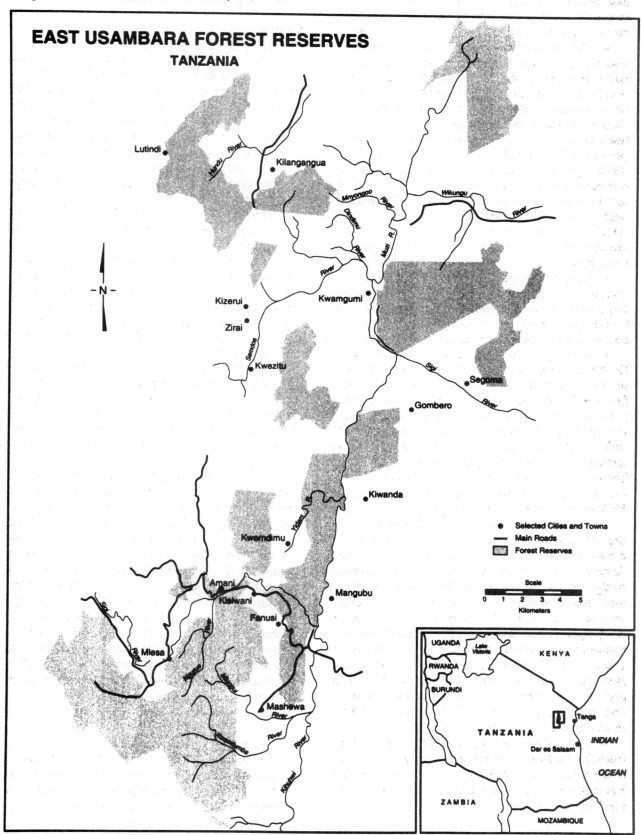

EAST USAMBARA FOREST RESERVES
TANZANIA

the regional resource functions, while adequately preserving the forests' biological diversity and environmental value." The project was implemented by the Ministry of Agriculture and Livestock Development, through the Tanga Regional Authorities, in collaboration with the Forestry Division and the International Union for Conservation of Nature and Natural Resources (IUCN). Thus the project was integrated with existing central and regional government institutions. The project received funding from the European Community (EC) through early 1990, and has received limited funds from other sources through June, 1992. The project applied for a three-year extension from the EC, but further funding is still uncertain.

In a separate initiative Finnida financed and conducted an inventory of the East Usambara forests in 1986 in collaboration with the Forestry Division, leading to the publication of a forest management plan in 1988. The management plan has not yet been implemented, and its future relationship with the project is unclear. The Finnish team summarized agriculture in the East Usambara as "a combination of decaying estates and ineffective, often unsustainable small-scale farming" (Finnida 1988, 1-11).

Project activities are directed by the project manager, a salaried employee of the Ministry of Agriculture and Livestock Development working with two expatriates—a technical adviser and an agricultural adviser. Other Tanzanian agricultural and forestry staff from the Ministries of Agriculture and Livestock Development and Lands and Natural Resources also work on the project as counterpart staff.

The area initially selected for attention by the project contains about 25,000 people, most of whom live within two days' travel of the project headquarters at Amani. To promote interaction with these communities the project selected a village coordinator from each of fifteen target villages. The regional government in Tanga pays their salaries and has guaranteed to make the positions permanent. The village coordinators are the primary link between the project and the villages. They are either trained by the project or sent to attend short courses. They meet monthly in Amani to report progress and problems. Many of the village coordinators have established agricultural demonstration plots in their own villages.

The project began in 1987, with an emphasis on three activities: surveying villagers, including extensive discussions with local people about project objectives; promoting substitutes for cardamom, including coffee, cloves, black pepper, cinnamon, pineapples, and sugarcane; and planting trees along the forest reserve boundaries.

The project now includes agricultural and rural development initiatives for protecting the forests, conserving soil, and generating income. The initiatives include establishing individual and village tree nurseries; contour planting, mainly with pineapples and guatemala grass; promoting women's activities, including a chicken-raising project, shops, commercial vegetable gardens, and a sewing project; establishing coffee nurseries in two villages; organizing village pit-sawing groups; establishing and stocking several fish ponds; assisting villagers with road repair and maintenance; distributing seeds and establishing private vegetable gardens; and stall-feeding livestock.

The project's first two years saw relatively little progress in getting people to work together effectively in planning or carrying out development activities. For example, pit sawing is one of the most lucrative local enterprises. Yet virtually none of the economic benefits from pit sawing are captured locally, and the project has had little success in encouraging local people to participate. Communal cash crop development at nurseries and other small-scale enterprises has also failed to attract support. This unwillingness to collaborate may spring from a lack of experience cooperating on joint ventures. Many of the villagers are comparatively recent migrants to the area, and consequently there are no traditions of community forest management in the area.

Evaluation and lessons

• The first two years of this project were mainly spent building and equipping the project center and staff housing. Implementation thus cannot yet be fully evaluated.

• Strong endorsement of the project by the Tanzanian government is indicated by participation by the Ministries of Agriculture and Livestock Development and Lands and Natural Resources, the placement of salaried ministry personnel in key project posts, and a guarantee of the permanence of the village coordinator positions. This commitment suggests that the activities have a good chance of being sustained, although continued external funding will be essential.

• The Forestry Division does not have enough personnel to enforce regulations in the forest reserves. Unless enforcement capacity is strengthened rapidly, the public land forests are unlikely to survive for long. However, the boundary tree planting activities promoted by the project are an important first step in conserving the forest reserves. By the end of 1989, 60 kilometers of the targeted 100 kilometers of boundary had been planted with trees.

• An effective community outreach mechanism was essential because of the large target population and the long travel time between villages. The village coordinator approach seems to be working well. The individuals selected as village coordinators seem dedicated to their work, and their active participation and high morale are evident at formal meetings and in communal village activities. With substantial support from the project leaders the village coordinators appear to have established constructive relationships with other villagers. The project appears to be highly regarded and its personnel well respected in the Amani region.

• Local participation in activities promoted by the project has included constructing fish ponds, planting trees to mark the forest boundaries, setting up private nurseries, and planting contour lines for soil conservation. Most of these activities were wage work, although some boundary tree planting was voluntary. The farming techniques promoted by the project have not been widely adopted, which is not surprising given the brief project history.

• Substantial data are available on the East Usambara forests, but no comparable baseline surveys have been carried out to describe the adjacent farming systems, which are one of the project's principal targets. The project's first agricultural adviser conducted a few preliminary and informal surveys, but they are incomplete. The lack of systematic agricultural and socioeconomic information creates two problems for project personnel, making it difficult for them to decide how to approach farming-system changes and, later, how to determine which changes in agricultural practices or socioeconomic variables are attributable to the project.

• An external evaluation of the project was carried out in 1989 by a team that included representatives from IUCN, the European Community, the Ministry of Agriculture and Livestock Development, the Forestry Division, and the Tanga Regional Authority. Recommendations included developing village woodlots as part of village land-use or resource-management plans. This would require more cooperation and planning among villagers than currently seems feasible. Part of the value in producing a land-use plan is that the process of preparing one and resolving the issues that arise can encourage participation by villagers in identifying and addressing collective problems. Imposing a plan from the outside or insisting that one be developed could be self-defeating. Villagers do not appear to consider fuelwood shortage as a major constraint, and it seems unlikely that this issue would catalyze interest in what could be a highly innovative collaborative venture.

• The project activities appear to have done much to gain the trust and respect of local people. This may not be "development," but it seems to be contributing to forging a relationship and creating an atmosphere that will promote the credibility—and possibly adoption—of future project initiatives.

• There is little evidence yet that conservation goals are being achieved; however, by the end of 1989 the project had probably done as much as, if not more than, could reasonably be expected.

Khao Yai National Park, Thailand

Context

The 2,200 square kilometer Khao Yai National Park is about 200 kilometers northeast of Bangkok (see map 3.3). It includes some of the largest remaining areas of tropical moist forest in mainland Asia and has exceptionally diverse plants and animals. For many rare species it is one of the last remaining viable habitats in Thailand. The park is also part of the hydrological cycle of northeast Thailand, containing the headwaters of four major rivers and supplying two large reservoirs. Khao Yai attracts 250,000-400,000 Thai and foreign visitors annually who spend 150 million baht ($5 million) on admission, lodging fees, transportation, food, and other services in the park (Dixon and Sherman 1990). The annual budget for park management is approximately 3.5 million baht ($120,000).

Land surrounding the park has been almost entirely deforested in the last three decades. The park is under pressure from illegal hunting and logging and from large-scale development projects—including some tourist facilities—that are incompatible with its protection function.

About 53,000 people live in 150 villages around the park. Most illegally occupy land classified as reserved forest (as do more than 7 million Thai villagers throughout the country). Limited and sporadic park enforcement measures have generated hostility and armed clashes between local villagers and personnel of the National Parks Division

Map 3.3 Khao Yai National Park, Thailand

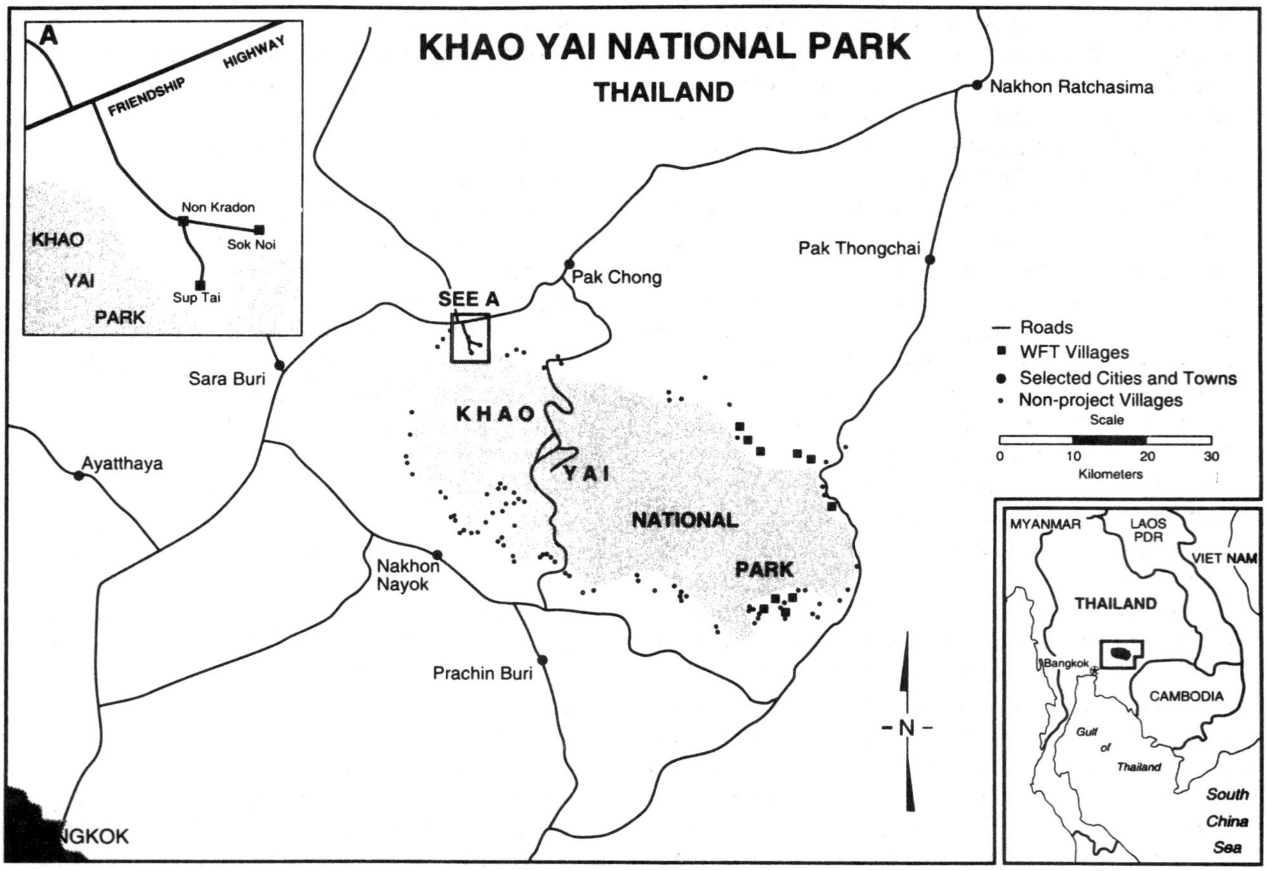

of the Royal Forestry Department; people on both sides have been killed. However, illegal activities in the park have continued, mainly poaching and logging.

Project

In 1985 two Thai nongovernmental organizations—the Population and Community Development Association and Wildlife Fund Thailand—began working together in Sup Tai village just outside the park boundary. The Population and Community Development Association, the largest nongovernmental organization in Thailand, has been organizing rural development programs emphasizing community participation since 1974. Its activities have reached more than 16,000 villages and have led to improvements in health, family planning, and income in many poor rural communities. Wildlife Fund Thailand, founded in 1983 and now a World Wildlife Fund-International affiliate, is a relatively small conservation organization that achieved prominence by attracting attention to

some of Thailand's most important environmental issues. It had no previous experience in project implementation.

A preliminary survey found that Sup Tai villagers were poorer than average and heavily in debt. Health and sanitation levels were low. There were no formal village institutions, literacy was rare, and a third of the villagers—mainly recent immigrants—had no legal land titles. The survey revealed that middlemen (loan sharks) controlled village economies, providing credit to farmers at a usurious 5 percent a month and then taking over the lands of those unable to repay the loans. As in many other rural areas of Thailand, the heavy indebtedness of villagers, who had no access to alternative credit sources, appeared to be the major constraint to change. Many villagers acknowledged illegally hunting and logging in the park.

The Sup Tai Rural Development for Conservation Project, which began in 1985, sought to find ways to conserve the park's natural resources while promoting improved income-generating opportunities. The project was built around a new village-level institution, the environmental protection society. An elected village committee administers the society with supervision from a full-time project manager. The environmental protection society was established as a vehicle for enabling villagers to make decisions and, eventually, to become financially and organizationally self-sufficient and independent from the project.

The most important project activity has been to provide loans to environmental protection society members from a revolving loan fund, in exchange for commitments to abide by park regulations. Interest rates on the loans were set at commercial bank levels—1 percent a month. From 1985 to 1989, 436 loans totaling about 2.1 million baht ($75,000) were made to Sup Tai residents. The loans have been repaid in full and on time, almost without exception. Early in 1990, the Bank of Agriculture and Agricultural Cooperatives agreed to provide credit directly to Sup Tai farmers on an experimental basis.

Other conservation and development activities have also been promoted, including soil conservation, livestock and fish raising, fruit tree cultivation, cooperative stores, improved sanitation and health practices, and a small park trekking program for tourists. Education programs have been designed to improve environmental awareness and to inform villagers of park regulations. Trees have been planted in the hills above the village to mark the park boundary.

In 1987 Wildlife Fund Thailand withdrew from the project to initiate the Environmental Awareness and Development Mobilization (TEAM) project in ten villages on the opposite side of the park, with conservation education activities in another forty villages. The Population and Community Development Association continued working in Sup Tai, expanded into two nearby villages during 1987, and had extended into three more by 1991. Both the new project and the expansion of the other projects are based on the Sup Tai model. The National Parks Department has had very little involvement in either of the projects.

A project manager from the Population and Community Development Association has been on-site at Sup Tai since 1985, employing a few local staff. Since 1987 this manager has also supervised project activities in the nearby villages of Non Kradong and Sok Noi. Wildlife Fund Thailand has two on-site project managers, one responsible for each group of five villages.

Funding for the Sup Tai project (1985-90) came from Agro Action, a German foundation, which provided 5 million baht ($180,000), and the Population and Community Development Association, which gave one million baht ($36,000). For the TEAM project USAID provided a three-year grant of 5.3 million baht ($190,000) but discontinued its funding early in 1990 after Wildlife Fund Thailand declined to increase the project scope to include more villages.

The project has brought major changes to Sup Tai. Early on, the project attracted national and international attention, culminating in a visit from the prime minister in 1987. The announcement of this visit led the province to carry out road improvements that dramatically reduced the travel time from Bangkok. Two years later, in another significant event for the village, Sup Tai was connected to the country's electricity network. These changes, which resulted from but were not encouraged by the project, have already altered the villagers' economic situation. The road improvement appears to have contributed to the rapid penetration of a cash economy and soaring land prices, both of which the villagers see as benefits.

Evaluation and lessons

• Villagers and officials assert that illegal activities continue throughout the park, mainly hunting and logging, although the projects have led to improved relations between villagers and park personnel. The overall project goal of strengthening protection for Khao Yai National Park has not been achieved, even in the area immediately around Sup Tai or the other project villages. A significant exception is that agricultural encroachment around Sup Tai ended after trees were planted to mark the boundary.

• The loan programs provide important economic benefits to villagers, although not yet on a scale large enough to enable them to become independent of the middlemen.

• The credibility of the environmental protection society as a viable organization separate from—if clearly related to—the projects has been emphasized. To some extent the project's sustainability depends on having the society continue after the nongovernmental organizations withdraw. Yet even the Sup Tai environmental protection society is not likely to become self-sufficient soon, contrary to earlier predictions.

• Funneling the loans through the environmental protection society was the major incentive for villagers to participate in the institution and to support the project's conservation goals. There is little evidence that villagers perceive the planned connection between the availability of credit through the environmental protection society and reduced illegal activities in the park. The implication is that the projects have not yet effectively linked their development activities and their conservation objectives. This is admittedly difficult to assess because the villagers' role in illegal activities in the park—before or now—is unknown.

• Apart from the loans, economic benefits flowing from the projects are difficult to identify and measure. Whether these benefits are enough to reduce the incentive to use natural resources from the park is questionable. Farming that emphasizes soil conservation and new crop varieties has had some success, mainly in Sup Tai, but adoption is not yet widespread.

• The partnership between the two project organizations provided a valuable opportunity to link expertise in conservation and development. The Population and Community Development Association has been able to draw on its well-established community-development and family-planning programs and could play a significant role in future replication of the Sup Tai model at other protected area sites. For Wildlife Fund Thailand, a relatively small organization, the TEAM project constitutes a considerable administrative burden. The split between the two organizations has unfortunately resulted in a loss of balance in the projects, with the Population and Community Development Association giving less emphasis to the effect of its activities on the park and Wildlife Fund Thailand making relatively little progress on the development aspects.

• Both organizations have learned that staffing is critical to maintaining progress. The Population and Community Development Association is a large and well-established organization, with a large supply of trained and experienced personnel. Wildlife Fund Thailand has an extremely small staff and little experience in project management. It has also had difficulty finding, hiring, and retaining suitable project field staff. The TEAM approach of two project managers, each covering five villages, appears to stretch limited resources too thinly.

• Except for the loan program, the willingness of local people to participate in project activities is closely related to villagers' personal reactions to the project staff. Project personnel in place at the end of 1989 all appeared to be capable, enthusiastic, dedicated, and highly respected by the villagers.

• Electrification and road improvement have had a profound effect on Sup Tai. Land prices increased at least sixfold from 1985 to 1989. Many farmers have been unable to resist these prices and have sold their land, becoming renters or moving elsewhere. Others have been forced to give up their land in lieu of debt repayments and have remained as renters or hired laborers or have joined Thailand's growing migratory rural population. The number of absentee landlords has increased considerably. This pattern appears to have been repeated at several sites around the National Park, particularly those within reach of major highways. The effects of these trends on the national park and on the conservation objectives of the projects are impossible to predict. In certain areas these effects are likely to escalate on a scale that may swamp any economic benefits of the projects. This illustrates the difficulty of predicting the effects of local development initiatives on parks.

• Evaluations carried out by the Population and Community Development Association's research and evaluation division have provided valuable inputs to the management of the various projects. These evaluations have included extensive interviews with villagers.

• Despite widespread, favorable attention to the projects around Khao Yai, there is no indication that any Thai government agency or nongovernmental organization plans to replicate this approach on a larger scale elsewhere. The National Parks Division is desperately short of resources, and its staff have neither the training nor the experience needed for a community development or extension program. The staff also lack the jurisdiction to operate outside national park boundaries. Its parent agency, the Royal Forestry Department, has to confront the reality of millions of people living illegally on reserve forest lands throughout Thailand, of which only a small fraction adjoins national park and wildlife sanctuary boundaries.

• Many of the villages around Khao Yai have now been reached in one way or another by the two projects. Only in Sup Tai, however, have any of the activities been operating long enough to be evaluated, and in Sup Tai they are in danger of being overwhelmed by the effects of road building and escalating land prices. Even in Sup Tai the precise nature of the project's successes and their implications for replication are elusive. Project activities in most of the other villages are too recent to have had an effect on park uses. Despite the many impressive aspects of the ICDP initiatives around Khao Yai National Park, there are few signs that the park deterioration is being stopped.

4. Implementing integrated conservation-development projects

Earlier chapters discussed the concept of integrated conservation-development projects (ICDPs) and described some of the projects. This chapter looks at the ICDP approach in more detail and analyzes the most innovative components. ICDP operations as a whole cover three areas:

- *Protected area management.* This area, where conservation activities are dominant, has been thoroughly discussed in the conservation literature, and discussion here is limited.
- *Buffer zones around protected areas.* An attempt is made to clarify this ambiguous notion, leading to the conclusion that buffer zones are a significant component in few, if any, of the case study projects.
- *Local social and economic development.* This is the innovative and most challenging aspect of ICDPs, and most of the chapter concentrates on this topic. The discussion highlights the magnitude of the challenge confronting ICDP managers and identifies several important issues that the case study projects have not yet addressed explicitly. A subset of the development component with more limited aims, the compensation and substitution approach, is also discussed.

By definition, the development component separates ICDPs from other conservation projects. For an ICDP to achieve its biodiversity conservation goals, however, it is not enough for the development component to foster improved local living standards—a difficult enough task. The development process must not only be economically and biologically sustainable, but must also conserve the ecosystem of the protected area. To satisfy this exacting requirement, explicit *linkages* between projects' development components and conservation objectives are needed.

Protected area management

ICDP activities in a traditional park—or the fully protected zone of a multiple-use area—are likely to emphasize biological resource inventories and monitoring, patrolling to prevent illegal activities, infrastructure maintenance, applied biological research and, possibly, conservation education. These activities are essentially similar to traditional-park management activities and have been well described elsewhere (for example, MacKinnon and others 1986; Miller 1978). (The constraints facing existing park agencies and their relative lack of effectiveness are discussed in chapter 7.)

Buffer zones

Managers of protected areas are well aware of the buffer zone concept. Management plans for traditional parks and multiple-use areas frequently refer to buffer zones, and several national conservation strategies have promoted the idea. Buffer zones have become so popular, in fact, that they are part of virtually all proposals for protecting natural areas.

Despite their intuitive appeal, however, buffer zones have not been adequately defined, and there are few working models. The term has been used to describe almost any initiative involving people that takes place near a protected area. As a result, there is a lack of consensus on issues involving buffer zones—their objectives, their location, whether they should be inside or outside parks, what criteria should determine their area, shape, and permitted uses (Wind and Prins 1989).

Buffer zones first received widespread attention as a result of UNESCO's Man and the Biosphere Program, which featured buffer zones as a key component of biosphere reserve models. The program was the first attempt to link protected areas with local social and economic development. The results from more than a decade of program implementation have been unconvincing, however (box 4.1).

Several definitions of buffer zones have been proposed. In an influential book that emerged from

---

Box 4.1 UNESCO's **Man and the Biosphere Program**

The biosphere reserve concept of the Man and the Biosphere Program first appeared in 1979, emphasizing the value of incorporating the needs and perceptions of local people in the establishment and management of reserves. The model biosphere reserve was described as consisting of a protected core area surrounded by a buffer zone and then a transition area. In the model, use of the buffer zone was limited to activities compatible with the protected core area, such as certain research, education, training, recreation, and tourism. Development activities involving local communities were intended to take place in the transition area (Batisse 1986). In later versions of the model the buffer zone and the transition areas were renamed the inner and outer buffer zones, although their functions were unchanged.

There are about 300 biosphere reserves worldwide. Comparisons between particular reserves and the model usually show that the distinction between the inner and outer buffer zones has blurred or disappeared, and little attention has been paid to promoting development in the buffer areas. Although the program has helped highlight the need to consider the relationship between protected areas and local people, the program has not demonstrated workable approaches.

One reason for the program's disappointing results is that most biosphere reserves were superimposed on existing parks and reserves (Hough 1988a). The agencies responsible for managing these areas usually lacked the resources, inclination, or ability to modify their management approach. As a result, the change of status to a biosphere reserve was in name only, with little change in emphasis or management philosophy. (This experience corresponds with the problems facing traditional parks described in chapter 2.)

---

the 1982 World Parks Congress, MacKinnon and others (1986, 90) offered the following:

> Areas adjacent to protected areas, on which land use is partially restricted to give an added layer of protection to the protected area itself while providing valued benefits to neighboring rural communities.

These authors emphasize that first priority should be given to protecting the park or reserve, and that benefiting local people is a secondary function.

Buffer zones tend to be conceived as relatively narrow strips of land on park boundaries, within which the "sustainable" use of natural resources will be permitted. The activities envisioned for buffer zones usually include hunting or fishing using traditional methods, collecting fallen timber, harvesting fruit, seasonal grazing of domestic stock, and cutting bamboo, rattan, or grasses. Activities forbidden in buffer zones generally include burning vegetation, cutting live trees, constructing buildings, and establishing plantations.

A variety of spatial patterns and arrangements for buffer zones have been described (see, for example, Lusigi 1981, MacKinnon and others 1986, Van Orsdol 1988). Few of these descriptions are based on working examples, probably because these are so rare. Although conservation biologists have given extensive consideration to the appropriate shape and size of protected areas, relatively little consideration has been given to the factors that would determine whether buffer zones should be inside or outside park boundaries, or how far the zones should extend.

Biological and social benefits have been claimed for buffer zones (box 4.2). The biological benefits are readily apparent. Most result from the fact that a buffer zone effectively expands the protected area by keeping major human impacts at a greater distance than would a conventional boundary.

The social benefits from buffer zones are more questionable. The sustainable use of wild plant and animal species would require a determination of sustainable exploitation limits for a variety of species, which is likely to be very difficult. Tropical ecosystems are extremely complex, and the long-term effects of removing single, let alone multiple, species are not well understood. Even where sustainable use levels could be determined for a variety of species with reasonable certainty, complex regulatory and enforcement mechanisms would presumably be required to ensure that these limits were not exceeded. It is not clear who should be responsible or how such limits might be enforced. While it is possible that local communities would perceive a self-interest in keeping buffer zone exploitation sustainable, there is little evidence to support such an assumption.

Another potential social benefit from buffer zones—providing a mechanism by which local people can genuinely benefit from the existence of a protected area—must also be carefully qualified. For example, it may be difficult to convince local people that restricted buffer zone access constitutes a valuable benefit if they had unrestricted use of the area prior to establishment of the protected area or if the proposed buffer zone area has already been degraded. Both of these situations are common on traditional park boundaries.

Another type of benefit that local people might derive from buffer zones would be some measure of protection from wildlife depredation. In parks

---

Box 4.2 Benefits of buffer zones

Biological benefits
- Provide a physical barrier to human encroachment into the strictly protected core zone.
- Provide extra protection from storm damage and micro-climate variation in small reserves.
- Enlarge the effective area of natural habitat of the reserve and reduce species loss through edge effects.
- Extend the habitat—and thus the population size—of large, wide-ranging species.
- Enhance the environmental services provided by the reserve—for instance, by protecting watersheds and by contributing to climatic regulation.

Social benefits
- Promote the sustainability of use of wild plant and animal species by local communities, thus safeguarding supplies of medicinal plants and wildlife for hunting.
- Provide a mechanism by which local people can genuinely benefit from the existence of a protected area and thus foster local interest in supporting conservation.
- Compensate local people for loss of access to the core-area resources.

Source: Poore and Sayer (1987).

---

where large-mammal populations have expanded because of effective protection, the animals often pose substantial threats to local people's crop fields, their livestock, and even their lives.

Overall, one of the most serious problems with buffer zones is the implication that the limited benefits that can flow to local people can change their behavior, reduce pressure on the plants and animals in the protected area, and thereby enhance the conservation of biological diversity. It is difficult to find logical reasons for this expectation. In a review of projects for the International Union for Conservation of Nature and Natural Resources (IUCN), Oldfield (1988, 1) found few examples of buffer zone management programs that "have succeeded in establishing stable and compatible land use systems around a protected area in such a way that local people are genuinely reconciled to the conservation function of the area."

In an attempt to increase the utility of the concept, Wind and Prins (1989) recently defined park buffer zones simply as areas outside of parks that are designed to protect parks. This approach gives renewed emphasis to protection, firmly relegating the supply of economic benefits to local people to a secondary role, to be implemented wherever possible. Even using this simple definition, the difficulties in establishing and regulating appropriate exploitation regimes are still likely to pose serious constraints on implementation.

Following the conservation literature and the approach taken in most protected area management plans, this study distinguishes buffer zones from other ICDP development components by the zone's principal emphasis on park protection, which relegates the supply of local economic benefits to a secondary role, and by their focus on specifically designated areas of land along protected area borders.

Under this interpretation, the game management areas around South Luangwa National Park in Zambia (box 4.3) were the only operating buffer zones among the case study areas. Although buffer zones had been legally established in the Annapurna Conservation Area in Nepal, on the borders of Gunung Leuser National Park in Indonesia, and at the Monarch Butterfly Overwintering Reserves in Mexico, none was functioning at the time of our study.

The case study projects show a large gap between buffer zone planning and reality. This is at least partly because most protected area management agencies have no legal authority to establish or manage buffer zones—outside or inside park boundaries. The governments of Nepal and Indonesia are currently considering appropriate legislation.

To sum up, current buffer zone definitions are inconsistent and overlook practical problems, and this precludes their implementation in all but very limited circumstances. The buffer zone concept, although deceptively simple and intuitively very appealing, thus faces considerable challenges. It remains, however, a high priority for many conservation programs, a key component of traditional-park management plans, and a potentially important ICDP component.

Local social and economic development

Promoting social and economic development among communities adjacent to protected area

27

Box 4.3 Lupande/Administrative Design for Game Management Areas (ADMADE), Zambia

The game management areas can be thought of as large buffer zones surrounding many of Zambia's national parks. Wildlife is strictly protected inside national parks. However, the entire Lupande/ADMADE project depends on revenues from hunting in the game management areas. Because a revenue-sharing system was instituted to provide local communities with proceeds from concession and hunting-trophy fees, local people suddenly had an important economic interest in preserving wildlife in their immediate area. As a result, poaching has been virtually eliminated from the game management areas because of the villagers' vigilance. Wildlife populations in some game management areas now exceed those inside some national parks.

---

boundaries is the central concern of ICDPs, clearly distinguishing them from other conservation projects. This is a new, highly complex, and challenging task for conservation practitioners. It introduces them to rural development, a field with an immense analytical literature and decades of field experience, much of it disappointing.

Approaches to overcoming or mitigating rural poverty vary according to perceptions of the underlying causes. The linkages are complex, variable, and not well understood. For example, the fact that poverty and environmental degradation are often found in close proximity should not necessarily be taken as evidence of causality in either direction (Jagannathan 1989). This argues for humility and flexibility in ICDP design and implementation. To reemphasize the conclusion of chapter 2, adequate knowledge of local social, economic, biological, and cultural factors that shape resource-use patterns is an essential prerequisite to using economic development to change these patterns to more park-friendly activities.

A recent World Bank survey (1990, 38) of what is known about the poor points to two "overwhelmingly important determinants of poverty,"

...access to income-earning opportunities and the capacity to respond. Where households are confronted with opportunities to use their labor to good purpose, and where household members are skilled, educated and healthy, minimum standards of living are assured and poverty is eliminated. Where such opportunities are not present, and where access to social services is severely limited, living standards are unacceptably low.

The rural development track record

The wise ICDP manager should surely become informed about some of the pitfalls that have beset past rural development projects, and—most important—be aware of the approaches that seem to offer the greatest promise of future success.

For example, starting with the experience of the major international development agencies, the World Bank and many of the bilateral donors of the Organisation for Economic Co-operation and Development dramatically expanded their lending for rural development projects in the 1970s. The projects were directed toward smallholders with their own land; only incidental benefits were planned for the "poorest of the poor"—laborers and the landless without productive assets (World Bank 1988, 8). According to a World Bank policy paper of 1975, the objectives of the projects included improved productivity, increased employment and thus higher incomes for target groups, and minimum acceptable levels of food, shelter, education and health. These projects thus bear comparison to ICDP development components.

It has long been apparent that many of the gains from these rural development projects were not sustained after project completion. In fact, many projects were later judged failures (Lewis 1988). A World Bank evaluation suggested that despite serious mistakes in the past, the general approach could still succeed (1988). But the report also called for substantial changes in rural development projects that amounted to a new model of development. Even in the best circumstances, the report warned, rural development projects can be expected to be expensive, lengthy, and difficult, with a high failure rate.

These were the key lessons:

• Rural development was most successful when government commitment to the projects was strong.

• When appropriate national policies are absent, the ability to sustain even successful projects is doubtful. The larger policy environment was perhaps the single most important factor affecting project success or failure.

• Sociological studies were inadequate for use

in rural development planning, especially in relation to the beneficiaries' social, economic, and cultural characteristics.

• Many integrated projects were too ambitious and complex, often placing impossible demands on local leadership and institutions. As a result, the projects performed more poorly than those with simpler designs.

• Projects with independent management units outside regular administrative structures sometimes helped achieve short-term objectives, but at the expense of needed long-term institution building.

• Reliance on expatriate technical assistance can enhance project implementation but shifts emphasis away from human capital development.

• There was a common failure to involve potential beneficiaries in the identification and design of projects. As a result, the beneficiaries had little stake in sustaining the projects.

• Production components require locally proven technical innovations, which are often not available.

• Monitoring should be routine, with evaluation conducted as an occasional special exercise.

Reports by or about other large development agencies generally tell a similar story. Yet—to briefly preview the case study findings—most of the ICDPs showed no evidence of having absorbed more than one or two of these lessons.

At the same time, although the earlier rural development projects and ICDPs have similarities, some clear distinctions can be drawn. Most obvious, many of the international agencies' rural development projects were significantly larger, more complex, and supported by financial resources of a magnitude greater than any ICDP. In addition, many of the rural development projects were implemented directly by government agencies, but ICDPs have been managed by different types of organizations, including local, national, and international nongovernmental organizations.

The large-agency integrated rural development projects have been criticized for being too "top-down." Top-down projects establish centralized decisionmaking bureaucracies that fail to involve—or be sensitive to the interests of—stakeholders (the intended project beneficiaries). Such projects also rely too much on project "blueprints" that demand adherence to a rigid—and usually short—project cycle. As Korten has pointed out (1979, 18), where knowledge is nearly nonexist-

ent, the blueprint approach calls for behaving as if it were nearly perfect, and although there is a need for "a close integration of knowledge building, decision making, and action taking roles, [the blueprint approach] sharply differentiates the functions....of the researcher, the planner and the administrator."

A "bottom-up" model of development has emerged more recently and has been strongly promoted and tested by development nongovernmental organizations such as the Aga Khan Foundation, CARE, the Ford Foundation, and World Neighbors. As the antithesis of the top-down model, the bottom-up approach emphasizes building slowly from a small scale, with flexible and adaptive project management, learning by doing, and involving stakeholders in all stages of a project cycle.

The literature describes different models of rural development and the considerable controversy surrounding evaluations of their relative effectiveness. In general, the organizations implementing ICDPs—particularly the nongovernmental organizations—have been more influenced by the bottom-up approach. (The extent to which rural development approaches have contributed to ICDP achievements is described in later chapters.)

The case study ICDPs that include rural development components—most of them small scale—include East Usambara (Tanzania), Khao Yai (Thailand), and Talamanca (Costa Rica), described in detail in chapter 3. Others include Air-Tenere (Niger), Andohahela and Beza Mahafaly (Madagascar), Annapurna (Nepal), Boscosa (Costa Rica), Central Selva (Peru), Lupande/ADMADE and the Luangwa Integrated Rural Development Project (Zambia), and Monarch and Sian Ka'an (Mexico) (see appendix).

There is an important distinction between the objectives of ICDPs and of rural development projects, regardless of whether the latter's methods are top-down or bottom-up. Although rural development projects seek to improve living standards and mitigate poverty, ICDPs aim to conserve biological diversity in protected areas. The ICDPs are therefore attempting to use rural development as a *means* of achieving this goal. This fundamental distinction adds a layer of complexity to the design and implementation of ICDPs for which there are few, if any, useful precedents. It is not enough, then, for the social and economic development components of ICDPs to avoid the pitfalls of rural development; the ICDPs must also organize their activities to enhance—or at least not threaten—nearby protected areas.

Compensation and substitution

One subset of the ICDP development component can be identified, with rather more modest goals. The aim here is to compensate local people for economic losses caused by the establishment of a protected area; provide substitutes for resources to which access has been denied, such as meat, timber, and grazing land; or provide alternative sources of income through new economic activities.

This approach can be justified based on the simple equity argument: that local people should not have to make economic sacrifices to protect an area established to provide *global* benefits (by conserving unique and valuable genes, species, and ecosystems). It also can be argued that providing appropriate compensation or substitutes can remove the economic incentive to illegally exploit a protected area's natural resources. The latter argument is intuitively very appealing but whether compensation and substitution can remove the incentives to exploit in unclear.

The compensation and substitution components are likely to be oriented toward people living in the immediate vicinity of a traditional park instead of, for example, people living in regional urban areas who buy and sell natural products such as fuelwood that were collected from the protected area. Benefits are thus directed toward actual or potential *agents* of park depletion, and not to the ultimate sources of demand for the resources.

Compensation is relatively simple, at least in theory, and could be in cash payments, goods, or services. These could be provided in exchange for agreements by local people to relinquish their former rights of access and to respect the conservation goals of the protected area. Substitutes can be targeted on specific resource uses. For example, if a protected area was formerly used as a source of fuelwood, woodlots outside the boundaries might provide an adequate substitute. If a traditional park was formerly used to graze livestock, water points (in arid areas) or stall-feeding (in wet areas), for example, could be substituted.

Direct substitutes may not be available outside the protected area, or may not be consistent with the area's objectives. For example, if a traditional park represents the only local source of construction materials, medicinal plants, certain fruits, or rare animal species, substitutes probably cannot be provided for individuals formerly dependent on these sources. But an ICDP could provide alternatives that attempt to increase incomes, reduce costs, or provide access to new ways of earning a living. These alternatives might include direct employment, low-interest loans, fertilizer subsidies, improved access to markets, promotion of nonrural enterprises, new skills training, and so on. Serious practical issues are likely to arise in determining who should benefit, the form of substitution, and what the total value of the substitutes should be.

As with buffer zones, compensation and substitution are intuitively appealing and have a certain simplistic logic. And, as with buffer zones, there are substantial obstacles to practical implementation. The key questions for ICDP compensation and substitution strategies are *who* should benefit, by *how much*, and for *how long*.

Addressing these questions requires identifying the appropriate community forum and making the case that continued compensation, substitution, or both depend on effective conservation of the protected area.

For compensation or substitution to be effective, some form of explicit agreement is desirable. It should specify the rights and obligations of the respective parties—the local people and the ICDP or protected area managers. The agreement should also be supported by enforceable penalties that provide enough incentive for both sets of parties to comply. Although theoretically plausible, such agreements are extremely rare. Local people, in particular, usually have no recourse.

Four ICDP case studies included components that used compensation or substitution (box 4.4). Agreements with local communities were reached at two sites, Amboseli National Park, Kenya, and Beza Mahafaly, Madagascar. At Amboseli, the government has failed to keep its side of the agreement for more than a decade. At Beza Mahafaly, the agreement has been maintained for several years through delicate negotiations with local and national politicians.

Need for linkages

This chapter has discussed three different components of ICDPs: protected area management, buffer zones, and local social and economic development. The activities in each of these components must be compatible with those of the other components—and consistent with a project's conservation goals. One of the most challenging tasks for ICDP manag-

---

Box 4.4 Case study projects using compensation or substitution

Amboseli, Kenya. In exchange for relinquishing access to the proposed national park, Masai pastoralists were promised compensation, some concession rights, and water points for their livestock in an arid area outside the park. After the park was established and a water piping system constructed, cutbacks in government funding ended the compensation payments and maintenance of the piping system. This system has now been inoperative for more than a decade. The pastoralists have continued to bring their cattle into the park, particularly during the dry season, thus competing with the large wild herbivores. Ironically, the continuing Masai presence appears to have discouraged poaching, which has devastated other parks in East Africa.

Annapurna, Nepal. Tourism had resulted in heavy fuelwood demands for cooking and for heating water, leading to rapid deforestation. Following negotiations, the owners of the many small lodges in the conservation area agreed to purchase kerosene stoves and to be bound by a regulation that fuelwood collection be limited to subsistence use. This measure has dramatically reduced the demand for fuelwood in the conservation area.

Beza Mahafaly, Madagascar. An agreement was reached between the project, the local population, and local political leaders to give up land for a small reserve in exchange for future development benefits, including an access road, an irrigation canal, and a school. While the canal is not yet working, the other activities have been implemented, some after long delays. Forest guards have been hired from local villages and the reserve is adequately protected. Local people have supported the project's conservation goals while receiving fairly modest development benefits in return. This appears attributable to the complete absence of government services in the area and a ten-year involvement of expatriates committed to a positive relationship with local communities and an effective dialogue with government agencies.

Chitwan, Nepal. In 1976 park authorities responded to local pressure by allowing villagers to collect tall grasses for house construction and thatching once a year from inside the national park, which is now the only remaining local source. This arrangement, which is at the discretion of the park authorities, restores a former practice that was interrupted when the park was established in 1973. While villagers benefit from this arrangement, rapid population growth and an acute shortage of resources have led to increased pressure on the park, which now relies for protection on 500 permanently deployed soldiers from the Nepalese Army.

---

ers is to promote development activities that not only improve local living standards but also lead to strengthened park management.

This goal can create difficult dilemmas for project managers. For example, building an access road may enhance local development by improving market access—but experience shows it may also improve park access for illegal hunting, timber cutting and settlement. Improving farming tools or introducing draft animals may allow farmers to increase productivity—but it may also free up labor, thereby leading to more land clearing and an expansion of the agricultural frontier. Agricultural development may principally benefit smallholders—but the rural landless may represent a greater threat to the park.

More generally, projects need to challenge the convenient and widespread—but totally unsupported—assumption that people made better-off by a development project will refrain from illegal exploitation of a nearby park in the absence of the negative incentive provided by more effective penalties. Such an expectation is naive; there is an

inescapable and widespread need to strengthen guard patrols and to impose penalties on those conducting illegal activities in parks. This is not inconsistent with the ICDP concept when such enforcement activities are integrated with genuine local development efforts and serious attempts to improve local people-park management communications through education campaigns.

These complexities all reemphasize the importance of linking the different components of an ICDP. A wide range of development activities can increase local incomes and living standards. What is less clear is how these and other project development components can be expected to enhance the conservation of biological diversity, particularly in the absence of more effective enforcement. During project design, very careful thought must be given to the anticipated linkages between the social and economic benefits for people living *outside* protected area boundaries and the needed behavioral responses to reduce pressure on resources *inside* the boundaries.

5. *Efforts to promote local development*

This chapter describes how the case study projects attempted to generate social and economic benefits for local people through (1) natural resource management outside core protected areas, (2) community social services, (3) nature tourism, (4) road construction for market access, and (5) direct employment. The chapter also briefly considers how these benefits were distributed—to individuals, groups, or communities—and whether the benefits have contributed to the integrated conservation-development project (ICDP) goal of conserving biological diversity.

Resource management outside protected areas

Most of the projects have attempted to encourage the use of improved natural resource management in and around their targeted communities, with two immediate objectives. The first was to increase the income of individuals or groups with natural resource ownership rights (or access) while conserving the natural resource base—soils, primary or secondary forests, fresh water, wildlife, and so on. The second was to encourage the substitution of more intensive production systems for existing extensive systems, thus reducing future pressure on protected ecosystems. Extensive systems are any form of logging, collection of fuelwood or other forest products, hunting, livestock grazing, shifting cultivation, slash-and-burn agriculture, or other uses that deplete the resources of an area, with the practitioners then moving on to new areas, a strategy that now only appears sustainable in the increasingly rare situation of population densities that are both low and stable.

In some case study areas, appropriate technologies for improved resource management were already known and used on a limited basis locally, in which case the ICDPs usually attempted to encourage adoption on a wider scale; in other areas, new technologies were needed. Technical options used in the case study projects included irrigation

works; new crop varieties and cultivation methods; soil treatments to reduce erosion, increase infiltration, and restore fertility; contour planting and maintenance of vegetation cover; energy saving to reduce fuel consumption; production of tree seedlings to provide fuelwood and construction materials; wells and boreholes for livestock in arid areas and stall-feeding in wetter areas; and low-intensity logging.

Resource management activities were concentrated in four sectors: agroforestry, forestry, irrigation and water control (for crops or livestock), and wildlife. In evaluating resource management within ICDPs, this study did not evaluate whether particular technical approaches were appropriate, except where such judgments were evident from the experience of the projects. The study was more concerned with identifying whether the technologies had been widely adopted, whether resource management practices had been intensified as a result, whether economic benefits had been generated locally, how the benefits were distributed, and whether protected area conservation was—or was likely to be—enhanced as a result (see the appendix to this chapter). The study recognized that although some of the ICDP activities had no direct link to conservation, they nonetheless played a valuable role in generating local popular support for the projects; and that some ICDPs have been operating for too short a time for positive results to be widely apparent.

The case study projects with resource management components make clear that local physical, ecological, and climatic conditions limit available technologies. Although technologies are increasingly available to enhance productivity and intensify land use in wet areas (World Bank 1990), options in dry areas are extremely limited (Nelson 1990). Few of the projects have allocated enough resources to carry out systematic experiments to identify new agricultural or agroforestry options, although some have established informal linkages to research institutes. Thus there is a lack of site-specific packages to provide alternative cultivation methods for the marginal lands at most of the case study sites. There has been little use of indigenous knowledge and technologies.

Land and resources in some areas have historically been abundant and readily accessible. People living near traditional parks that at least nominally protect relatively large areas of forest or other natural systems may believe this abundance continues, despite the outsider's view that only fragments of the original plant and animal species remain. In these circumstances the conservation or intensification of land-use practices is unlikely to be attractive to local residents. In the absence of other incentives, merely suggesting or demonstrating better resource management practices is unlikely to bring significant change. For example, farmers are unlikely to be unduly concerned about soil erosion—and prepared to invest valuable labor resources in controlling it—if they can burn and clear nearby forest land and continue extensive cultivation practices.

There is little evidence as yet among the case studies of widespread adoption of environmentally benign technologies with the potential to increase income or intensify land use. It is, however, too early to evaluate the projects that started comparatively recently, many of which are emphasizing agroforestry. In a few cases, projects have promoted alternatives before local people felt they were needed. Examples are the woodless house construction technique introduced at Air-Tenere. Although this knowledge may prove useful, few people as yet have adopted this construction technique.

It is evident that an appropriate framework of incentives must be established to encourage the adoption of new technical options or the continuation of sound existing practices. These incentives should be directed toward groups or individuals whose actions threaten the protected area. Incentives may be specifically designed to provide local people with income-earning opportunities that are contingent on respecting regulations in protected areas. They could include improved access to markets, low-interest credit, the clarification or reform of land tenure arrangements, shares of revenue from tourism and safari hunting, direct employment by the protected area or the ICDP, limited access to resources from within the protected area, and provision of community services.

To facilitate the identification, dissemination, and adoption of sound technical practices, appropriate social and institutional arrangements must also be established. These can include formal arrangements with government agencies responsible for programs such as agricultural research and extension, education, health care, wildlife, forestry, and so on. They also can include the establishment or modification of community organizations that can both mediate between villagers and outside bodies—such as government representatives and ICDP personnel—and make local resource management decisions.

Community social services

Several of the case study projects have provided—or supported the establishment of—basic social services in the communities they are targeting. These services have included school building construction, support for teacher salaries and equipment purchases, construction and support of health clinics, family planning, sanitation and nutrition programs, and a day care center. Although these types of services are more commonly provided by government, many of the communities targeted by ICDPs are in remote areas, beyond the reach of existing national programs.

As an ICDP component the provision of community-level social services can be a response to the expressed needs of a community—or it can be part of the compensation in exchange for setting aside protected lands or for cooperating with the project's conservation objectives.

Among the case study projects the most explicit compensation package was the agreement reached with the people of Beza Mahafaly, in Madagascar, which included providing a school and support for a teacher's salary. At Amboseli, in Kenya, a clinic was provided for the Masai as part of the agreement to establish the park, although alternate grazing lands were the pivotal issue. In the remaining cases, community social services were provided to improve local living standards, without direct or explicit conservation links.

Social services can be provided to communities under various arrangements. They may be given "free" by the project or as part of an agreement that includes other components—as at Beza Mahafaly. Or, a nominal fee may be charged those using the services. The services also may represent the outcome of a joint venture between the project and the community, requiring the community to contribute cash, labor, or other goods and services. The latter approach has been successfully adopted by the Annapurna project in Nepal (box 5.1).

Several questions arise when ICDPs provide community services. What kind of community services are appropriate in particular circumstances? Who selects the services—the project or the community? If the community, which members of the community make the selections? And who benefits? We look at these issues in the discussion of community participation in ICDPs in chapter 6.

Nature tourism

The benefits from all kinds of international tourism are of considerable interest to governments badly in need of foreign exchange. The economic benefits to be gained from tourism linked to natural areas—nature tourism—have long been recognized as significant for conservation. Nature tourism can generate benefits for conservation at several levels: by providing an economic return to the nation, it can justify setting aside large areas of land for conservation; entry fees can generate substantial funds to support management; and tourist expenditures (on lodging, transportation, food, guides, and souvenirs) can be an important source of income for communities nearby, compensating them for loss of access to traditional resources and giving them an incentive to conserve the wildlife. The case study ICDPs have promoted nature tourism to provide funds for protected area management and generate income gains for local communities. (For a more general discussion of nature tourism, see Boo 1990 and Lindberg 1991).

In economic terms, tourism is the most important activity in or around the case study sites at Air-Tenere (Niger), Amboseli (Kenya), Annapurna (Nepal), Chitwan (Nepal), Khao Yai (Thailand), Monarch (Mexico), and Volcanoes (Rwanda). The countries in which these case studies are located, plus Costa Rica, all generate substantial foreign exchange earnings from tourism associated with protected areas. Khao Yai and the Monarch Butterfly Overwintering Reserves also attract many domestic tourists.

The tourism components of the case study ICDPs have emphasized mitigating the environmental effects of tourism (Air-Tenere, Niger, and Annapurna, Nepal), increasing the economic return from tourism (Volcanoes, Rwanda), redirecting the economic benefits from tourism toward local people (Amboseli, Kenya, and Annapurna, Nepal), and conducting promotion and education activities for tourists (Monarch and Sian Ka'an, Mexico) (box 5.2).

The results thus far have been disappointing, to say the least. In general, all spending by visitors—on transportation, food, lodging, or even park entry fees—goes directly to the central treasury or to private corporate interests that have been granted concessions (Annapurna is an exception). At popular sites, tourism revenues greatly exceed protected area operating budgets. It is unusual for any of these revenues to be returned directly for park management and extremely rare for a revenue share to go to local people. For example, the value of visits by tourists to Khao Yai National Park in Thailand has been estimated at $5 million annually, which is about 100 times the national park budget; none of it goes to local people. The revenues from tourists visiting the mountain gorillas of Rwanda are returned to Volcanoes and other national parks in Rwanda but, again, local people do not participate in the benefits. In three case study projects, local people received some share of entry fees or amounts paid to concessionaires: Amboseli (Kenya), Annapurna (Nepal), and Monarch (Mexico). Some local employment opportunities were linked to tourism at Chitwan (Nepal) and Volcanoes (Rwanda), but these were insuffi-

---

Box 5.1 Local contributions to social services: The Annapurna project

The Annapurna Conservation Area project in Nepal has avoided investing in community projects as "gifts" and has consistently insisted on local participation, in cash or labor, in any community project. At least a 50 percent local contribution is usually planned, and wherever possible project inputs are limited to contributions in kind (such as purchased goods). This is based on the belief that when local people are interested enough in a venture to invest in it—as opposed to receiving a perhaps-unwanted gift—they will have a greater interest in ensuring that the venture succeeds.

On this basis, local people in the village where the project headquarters is located raised 100,000 NR ($5,000) as matching funds for a community health center, a process that took more than a year. For a local small-scale hydroelectric project, a Canadian donor provided 900,000 NR ($45,000) and the project provided 350,000 NR ($17,000). The panchayat (the local political organization) obtained and took responsibility for a five-year bank loan to cover the remaining 550,000 NR ($27,000). The owners of small tourist trekking lodges raised 50 percent of the cost of repairing and cleaning up the footpaths and trails in their area. This approach, although painstakingly slow, appears to be working extremely well and eliciting serious local consideration and participation. It may, however, be undermined by the eagerness of other donors to become involved in the conservation area and to make large grants to the communities—something local leaders are well aware of.

Box 5.2 Nature tourism

Air-Tenere Reserve, Niger. This area has become an increasingly popular attraction for European and North American tourists who cross the desert in all-terrain vehicles. The wildlife of the reserve are a primary attraction for tourists and, thus, are economically important. The development of a locally based tourist industry is recognized by the project as a potentially important long-term development strategy that, if properly controlled, may be made compatible with conservation objectives. The project is attempting to promote increased local participation in the tourist industry, which is currently dominated by tour operators located in Agadez, about 300 kilometers south of the reserve. The project has cooperated with local artisans in establishing a center for displaying and selling local arts and crafts.

Annapurna Conservation Area project, Nepal. Since Nepal was opened to foreign visitors in the 1950s, tourism has expanded rapidly to become the country's top foreign exchange earner. More than 30,000 trekkers visit the spectacular Annapurna area each year (its permanent population is 40,000). The growth in the number of visitors has led to a proliferation of small tea shops and trekking lodges along the trails but has had a substantial negative impact on the natural environment. Large areas of forest have been cut to provide cooking, heating, and lodging for visitors.

An early goal of the conservation project was to increase the local economic benefits from tourism and to reduce the environmental impact of trekkers. Training courses for the owners of lodges and tea shops have upgraded the quality of service, standardized menus and prices, and improved standards of sanitation and waste disposal. These successes have greatly enhanced the status and influence of the project locally. To conserve energy in the conservation area, lodges and expeditions are now required to use kerosene, with fuelwood collection being limited to subsistence use. The conservation project has provided expertise, but not financing, for lodge owners to install back boilers (which heat recycled water during cooking to conserve energy) and solar panels. Lodge owners have also contributed to the cost of trail upgrading and maintenance.

The value of the economic benefits being accumulated by lodge owners has not been estimated but is clearly considerable by local standards and has dramatically increased the average per capita income. The use to which this surplus is being put has not been monitored. Some lodge owners have bought land in the nearest town, Pokhara, while others send their children to better schools in larger towns. In the villages on the major trekking routes, the incomes of about 100 to 150 families owning tea shops or lodges have significantly increased in the last decade. However, employment for nonfamily members appears to be very limited, and with the notable exception of some seasonal vegetables, most supplies are bought from Pokhara, many originating from outside Nepal. Some goods are purchased from traders who move up and down the trails, and employment for porters has undoubtedly increased because all goods must be carried by hand. But the significant local economic benefits from tourism have not been distributed widely either among or within villages.

An entry fee to the Annapurna Conservation Area has been collected from visitors since 1989. The 200 rupee (NR, $8) fee, which required government approval, is yielding an annual revenue of 4 million NR ($160,000)—equal to half the revenues from all of the trekking permits issued in Nepal, or more than 40 percent of the revenues from all of the national parks combined. The revenues collected pass directly to the Annapurna Conservation Area project.

Royal Chitwan National Park, Nepal. Chitwan has grown in importance as a tourist destination since the first wildlife safari lodge was established in 1965. Seven high-cost tourist lodges now have licenses to operate in the park, and more than forty small ones have sprung up outside. The park entry fee is now 250 NR ($9). Trained elephants are used to transport people around the park from both areas. The number of visitors has risen steadily and seems likely to continue to grow. Except for the annual grass collection (see box 4.4 in chapter 4), the benefits flowing from the park to local people are minor. In contrast to Nepal's Himalayan parks, local people are only marginally involved in tourism in Chitwan park. While traders benefit, most people face higher local prices as a result of tourism.

Khao Yai, Thailand. Khao Yai has become a premier tourist destination since its establishment in 1962 as Thailand's first national park. During the 1980s the park attracted 250,000 to 400,000 Thai and foreign visitors annually. These visitors spend an estimated 150 million baht ($5 million) each year on admission, lodging fees, transportation, food, and other services within the park; the annual budget for park management is 3.5 million baht ($120,000). Virtually none of the revenue goes to people living in the villages surrounding the park. The Sup Tai project, in Sup Tai village next to the park (see chapter 3), includes a small jungle trekking program for visitors. This program attracts several groups each year to Sup Tai village, but the economic benefits generated are modest, even for one village.

Monarch Butterfly Overwintering Reserves, Mexico. The spectacular display of the Monarch butterflies provides a unique nature tourism opportunity. The reserves received nearly 100,000 visitors in 1989. Yet only one of the five reserve areas is equipped for tourism. The facilities include an interpretive trail and visitor center, with the nearest community receiving the entrance fees to use for community projects. The community also benefits from sales and employment generated by a small store that Monarca, A.C., the nongovernmental organization implementing the project, helped establish in 1986. Women from the community have put up stands to sell food to tourists. In general, however, tourism to the area is unregulated and disorganized. Benefits to the local community are unevenly distributed and offer insufficient incentive to stop deforestation. As employment in the area continues to decline, the unrealized conservation value of tourism increases while the tiny reserves continue to be logged.

Volcanoes National Park, Rwanda. The park's mountain gorillas are the nation's main tourist attraction. Prior to the start of the tourism component of the project in 1979, the park received about 1,200 visitors annually. Visits increased to nearly 5,000 in 1983 and more than 10,000 in 1989. This increase, combined with an increase in gorilla viewing fees (from $5 to $200 per person), has led to a thirtyfold increase in tourism revenues. Project staff have habituated gorilla groups to human presence, permitting the animals to be closely approached by tourists. Current direct tourism revenue at the park is about $1 million annually. A proportion of the proceeds are returned to conservation in Rwanda but none goes to local people. The government has recently put significant pressure on the project to allow more visits to the gorillas to earn higher revenues.

cient to attract much popular local support for the parks.

To summarize this rather bleak picture, a sentiment expressed by Hemanta Mishra (1984) of the King Mahendra Trust for Nature Conservation at the 1982 World Parks Congress bears repeating. Although he was referring specifically to Nepal's Royal Chitwan National Park, his thoughts are applicable to many conservation sites today:

> Our preoccupation with hopes that tourism will catalyze local support or change public attitudes seems to be self-defeating since the benefits from tourism were overplayed both by government authorities and tourist organizations.... The concept of selling the idea of a national park from the benefits to the local people from wilderness-oriented tourism has not been successful and is unlikely to have any positive impact within the next decade. (203, 207)

Even if the vast conservation benefits potentially available from nature tourism could be realized, it is important to remember that only a small minority of protected areas attract significant numbers of visitors. The characteristics of sites attracting large numbers of tourists include spectacular scenery, large mammals, uniqueness, reasonable access, and developed infrastructure (such as roads and accommodation facilities). The proportion of most countries' protected areas for which large-scale tourism is viable is thus extremely small. In particular, the potential for many tropical moist forest sites to attract large numbers of tourists is limited. For example, the Gunung Leuser and Dumoga-Bone National Parks in the Indonesian Outer Islands, which are biologically among the most important conservation sites in Southeast Asia, are unlikely ever to attract significant numbers of tourists. In Madagascar, the presence of rare and endangered species attracts small numbers of visitors to several tropical forest sites. This form of "ecotourism," or adventure tourism, can make modest contributions to local economies but does not have the potential to attract the volumes of tourists who flock to Nepal's Himalayan parks and the African wildlife parks.

Road construction for market access

Product marketing opportunities in remote rural communities tend to be limited by the difficulty of access to and from villages. Crops are therefore more likely to be selected for subsistence use and local exchange rather than for sale in small towns or other regional markets. In these circumstances it can be difficult to introduce new crops, new varieties, or new cultivation techniques that are less threatening to the environment without improving market access. Some of the case study projects attempted to improve market access through road construction and through the promotion of marketing associations (chapter 6).

Roads that provide or improve access to regional product and labor markets are highly valued and can serve as powerful incentives to the adoption of more intensive agricultural and forestry techniques. Although the distribution of benefits from improved market access varies by community, the economic situation of entire villages can improve significantly. The construction or improvement of access roads has had a substantial impact at several of the case study sites. In some cases these improvements were initiated by the projects, while in others they were unconnected.

At Beza Mahafaly, in Madagascar, villagers specifically agreed to the establishment of a reserve in exchange for external support for local development projects. Improvement of an access road to the nearest market town was a top priority. On a much larger scale, the Luangwa Integrated Rural Development Project (LIRDP) in Zambia includes a substantial road construction component. In Indonesia the irrigation projects linked to Dumoga-Bone National Park would have had little value without the improvement of a highway connecting the valley with nearby towns, enabling local rice surpluses to be exported.

However, roads can have other, less predictable effects on protected areas. As described in chapter 3, substantial road improvements at Sup Tai village on the border of Khao Yai National Park in Thailand have caused local land prices to soar, forcing indebted smallholders off the land and adding to Thailand's rapidly growing population of migratory landless. The effects of these changing land ownership patterns on the national park are impossible to predict.

Roads also can directly endanger conservation, as is readily evident in the Amazon. Gunung Leuser National Park, in Indonesia, has been cut in two as a result of the transformation of a rough seasonal road through the park into an all-weather highway. Settlers have expanded along the road from three small enclaves, removing timber and other forest products, burning, and planting annual crops. Gunung Leuser's species-rich lowland forests have now been degraded in a swath stretching for several kilometers on both sides of the road, essentially bisecting the park and threatening its ecological integrity.

All roads also open the possibility of increased inward migration, possibly by people attracted by the ICDP. Roads, in turn, facilitate the transport of illegal products—fuelwood, construction materials, or wildlife—from a protected area. As with many other ICDP interventions, road construction requires a mechanism to monitor effects and modify project approaches during implemen-tation.

Direct employment

The most direct source of income arising from an ICDP is a job with the project or with the protected area targeted by a project. All case study projects created at least some local employment, whether temporary or permanent. Positions included game scouts (in Africa), park wardens and guards, guides, community extension workers, administrative staff, cooks, manual laborers and construction workers, carpenters, and mechanics. The direct distribution of these benefits is obviously limited to the employees and their families, and depends on where they spend their wages.

The Administrative Design for Game Management Areas (ADMADE) program in Zambia supports 400 village scouts permanently. The Nazinga Game Ranch in Burkina Faso hired about 600 local people for about two years during the initial construction and has hired intermittently since then. No other projects have come close to matching this number of jobs, although many provided long-term employment for much smaller numbers. The project in the East Usambara Mountains in Tanzania hired fifteen village coordinators and trained them in extension work. The government has committed to hiring these individuals as permanent civil service employees after the project ends. Local hiring by the other projects has been limited.

Most project-related employment has resulted from specific needs related to construction, maintenance, accommodation, and so on. Job opportunities through the projects can create considerable local goodwill and can make a substantial economic contribution, particularly in the case of small communities. If the period of employment is limited by the length of the project, however, any conservation benefits are likely to be temporary. At this stage there has been little evidence of increased indirect employment arising from stimulation of local economies by any project.

Linking the benefits from development to conservation

The case study projects have brought benefits to local people, principally through income gains and improved access to social services. Some of these gains have been achieved by innovative project components implemented under challenging circumstances. From a strictly developmental perspective, several of the projects appear quite promising—and one or two very successful.

However, the goals of ICDPs are considerably more ambitious than to provide social and economic benefits. The ICDP approach has to be judged on whether development initiatives have contributed to improved management and security of a protected area, and whether local people have become reconciled to the existence of the protected area. The critical linkage between development and conservation is still generally missing or unclear. It is still doubtful that many ICDP-generated local benefits have reduced pressure on the areas the ICDPS are trying to protect.

Questions remain about the adequacy of the benefits generated, their distribution, and even their specific purposes. A key issue is the extent to which local people have participated in ICDP components designed to provide them with benefits. More than two decades of rural development experience suggests that project success is rarely achieved without local participation. These issues are discussed in greater detail in chapter 6.

Appendix. Natural resource management components of case study projects

Agroforestry

Annapurna Conservation Area project, Nepal. As part of efforts to combat deforestation, the first stage of this project included establishing several community nurseries and distributing tree seedlings free or at low cost. Farmers have been encouraged to plant trees to stabilize slopes and provide fuelwood and fodder. Although the demand for seedlings has been encouragingly high, there is little information on survival rates. It is thus difficult to know how effective the nurseries are. As predictions of local fuelwood deficits become more pessimistic, the successful promotion of high-altitude tree planting in the near future assumes critical importance. The project is also encouraging stall-feeding of livestock, a major shift in land use, which could focus greater attention on the production of fodder trees.

The second stage of the Annapurna project started in 1991 and emphasizes agroforestry as the main tool for boosting the incomes of the poor farmers who comprise the vast majority of the region's population. Possible technical solutions are to be worked out with assistance from outside experts and a local agricultural research station. This appears to be the best strategy in the absence of adequate resources to invest in infrastructure, such as hydroelectric power generation. But little is known about the farming systems now used or their potential for productivity improvements. There are few convincing examples of successful agricultural or forestry development in the Himalayas, and the Annapurna project faces a formidable challenge in attempting to significantly improve economic conditions for the region's farmers.

Bururi and Rumonge projects, Burundi. When the Bururi project began, logging and fuelwood collection for local use had already degraded part of this very small reserve, and pine plantations had been established inside the reserve. Project activities had initially emphasized the establishment of nurseries and plantations to produce exotic tree species, primarily pines. But a subsequent project evaluation pointed out that the plantation trees were of little economic interest locally, that the plantations had little conservation value, and that illegal exploitation of the reserve was continuing unchecked. In response the project reoriented its activities, hiring eleven guards and an agroforestry adviser led by a Peace Corps volunteer.

The guards sharply reduced reserve encroachment. Project personnel report that the wood biomass produced as a result of the project agroforestry activities has started to provide an alternate source to the reserve's trees. The government assumed financial responsibility for the project after USAID funding expired in 1987, by which time the project had distributed 250,000 seedlings to local farmers, consolidated reserve management and enforcement, and marked the reserve boundaries. Recent cutbacks in government support have led to problems such as an inability to buy plastic seedling bags, reducing the nurseries' distribution capacity.

The Rumonge project is attempting to replicate the Bururi experience around three small reserves, beginning with nursery establishment and agroforestry trials. By 1988 eight nurseries had been established and were producing more than 200,000 seedlings annually. At Bururi and Rumonge, local people appear to have benefited

from receiving or buying tree seedlings from the project nurseries, although some families have been relocated from the reserves. Increased enforcement appears to have been critical in reducing illegal logging and fuelwood collection.

East Usambara Mountains, Tanzania. Industrial logging was stopped before the project began. The major resource management challenge has been to introduce an effective substitute for the cultivation of cardamom, an important local income source and a major export crop, but one that degrades the soil and requires continuous forest clearing. Demonstration agroforestry plots have been established in several villages and project staff have worked directly with individual farmers to experiment with a variety of cash crops in combination with different tree species. The project has been operating for only two years and thus is not ready to be evaluated. However, despite clear local interest, there is no evidence that any of the new options are being widely adopted as cardamom alternatives.

Talamanca Region, Costa Rica. Small farmers throughout the region depended on cacao as a primary source of income until monilia pod rot, a fungal disease, devastated cacao production. ANAI, the local nongovernmental organization running the project, has promoted community-run nurseries in an attempt to introduce improved varieties of cacao and other agroforestry species, to establish a stable and diversified production base for local communities. ANAI reviews characteristics of species grown worldwide to identify those that are suited to the agroecological conditions in Talamanca. Tests for suitability are carried out on an experimental farm, and if successful, the plants are transferred to the nurseries. Local demand has been generated for one crop native to Brazil, previously unknown in Costa Rica, which produces a refreshing juice. Creating demand for such new products has proved difficult, however, because farmers prefer to plant cacao. They are familiar with it, a market—albeit weak—exists, it is easy to transport and store, and so on. Most of the forty community-run tree nurseries have planted improved cacao varieties.

Forestry

Boscosa, Costa Rica. Although this was conceived as a natural forest management project involving small farmers, it soon became apparent that the extensive resource degradation in the region, mainly from logging, combined with complex social and economic issues, would require a broader spectrum of activities. The project began to promote reforestation, ecotourism, management of the existing forest (as an alternative to cutting new forest) for timber and nontimber products (such as medicinal and ornamental plants), and improved agriculture and agroforestry in cleared areas capable of supporting agriculture. Natural forest management activities were set aside for the first two years of the project in favor of providing immediate and visible solutions to problems identified by local communities. The lack of clear technical options, especially of silvicultural techniques appropriate to local conditions, led the project to broaden its focus into agroforestry, agricultural development activities, reforestation, and community organization.

Central Selva, Peru. One of the goals of the project was to demonstrate that sustainable management of primary tropical forests is technically and economically viable, based on the strip shelterbelt system. Following forest inventories, long and narrow (20- to 40-meter wide) strips are clear-cut through existing forest, and logs are extracted by animal traction. All cuttings are used: small pieces for fence posts, larger sections for lumber, and scraps for charcoal. Natural regeneration reclaims the gaps, maintaining high levels of species diversity. The Amuesha Indians have now formed a forestry cooperative using this system on their lands, and have begun to demonstrate the system's technical viability. However, external factors, including violent civil unrest and severe economic problems, have caused delays. And the link between these activities and reduced encroachment in the park is unknown.

Sian Ka'an, Mexico. The objectives of the Pilot Forestry Plan (PFP) are to find the best land uses and harmonize the ecological equilibrium, to foster social participation in the productive process, and to improve and diversify horizontal and vertical integration of established industry. The project involves the participation of fifty-three *ejidos* (communities) and 9,000 families, or half of the rural households in the state of Quintana Roo.

PFP staff work with each ejido to develop a forest management plan based on local forest inventories, which ejido members are trained to carry out, including demarcation of a permanent forest area. The inventory results are entered into a computerized data base to produce maps and charts giving projected tree growth and potential harvesting levels. The PFP has assisted ejidos in organizing to obtain financing to purchase logging equipment, including saw mills, trucks, tractors,

and small tools—billing the ejido a percentage of the future harvest. Although the concept is promising, the PFP has not yet been able to fully realize all its aims since not all ejidos have a good endowment of valuable tree species.

Irrigation and water control

Air-Tenere National Nature Reserve, Niger. This massive multiple-use area is situated in an harsh environment on the southern fringes of the Sahara Desert. Rainfall is sporadic and averages less than 100 millimeters annually. The population of about 4,500 is concentrated in two settlements with year-round access to water. The project has established nurseries in both settlements. Windbreaks, tree stands, and six small experimental dams have been established in and around village gardens to contain soil erosion resulting from water runoff. The dams were very popular and another 662 dams were constructed during the following two years. By 1989 soil erosion had stabilized, vegetation growth had improved, and most of the gardens had benefited directly or indirectly from the protection afforded by the dam system. Teams of locally recruited laborers were employed to construct the dams. The project has also attempted to restore two degraded pastures, following requests from herders. At one of these sites the activity involves placing barriers to water courses (similar to long dams) to hold water over a longer period of time and reduce erosion.

The Air-Tenere conservation situation is unusual in that the threats to the reserve have come from tourism and poaching, the latter mainly by soldiers. The indigenous population does not hunt and is tolerant of wildlife. The publicity surrounding the project, the legal prohibitions against hunting, and the enforcement activities of project staff have largely eliminated poaching in the area as the protected area boundaries have come to be recognized and respected. Tourist activities are now controlled by recognized guides. Local residents pose a threat only during droughts, when their livestock tend to destroy the sparse vegetation needed by wild herbivores. The restrictions on destructive grazing in the new protected area remain largely untested because rainfall in the area has been normal in recent years.

Beza Mahafaly and Andohahela Reserves, Madagascar. As part of the original agreement to establish the small reserve at Beza Mahafaly, the project committed to rebuild an irrigation canal. For various bureaucratic, engineering, and financial reasons, this commitment has remained unfulfilled for more than a decade. Small agricultural demonstration plots have been established in one village close to the reserve to stimulate the cultivation of new cash crops. So far the results have been disappointing. Despite these setbacks the reserve is intact, and there appears to be substantial local political support for the project. The support appears to derive from the provision of a school, the continuing prospect of irrigation, and the attention given to villagers and local and national political figures by the project staff and associated researchers—Malagasy and expatriate.

At Andohahela, small-scale irrigation works have been introduced to expand irrigated areas in valley bottoms. Individual farmers in several villages have increased their incomes as a result of this program, despite some technical problems with dam and water channel construction. The conservation implications of this program and whether it is leading to intensified agriculture are unclear. In at least one case, expansion of his irrigated rice fields led a farmer to clear steep forested slopes adjacent to the reserve to be able to continue cultivating manioc and cassava.

Dumoga-Bone National Park, Indonesia. The development component of this major project in north Sulawesi has allowed more than 8,000 farmers to grow 10,000 hectares of irrigated rice. Establishment of the national park to protect the headwaters of the rivers supplying the irrigation systems was a condition of the $60 million World Bank loan for the projects. The farmers who benefited were almost entirely migrants and transmigrants from Java and Bali who were already familiar with the cultivation of paddy rice. They have derived considerable economic benefit from the project, and the region has recently become a net rice exporter for the first time. This project has undoubtedly been successful in increasing farmer incomes, stimulating the regional economy, intensifying agriculture, stabilizing land use, and linking a national park to an economic development initiative. It also represents one of the more impressive transmigration projects in Indonesia. However, the effective protection of the park is primarily attributable to the cancellation of logging concessions and strict enforcement, the latter facilitated by a substantial park operating budget and local government cooperation. The rice farmers presumably have little interest in clearing forest land and have enough income to make encroachment unattractive; the original Dumoga Valley inhabitants, who lived in and around the forest, gave up or were forced off their land by the project. They were prevented from clearing new agricultural sites by the park guards and ultimately were forced to disperse to other areas.

Wildlife

Lupande Development project and ADMADE, Zambia. Legislation under colonial rule turned over wildlife ownership to the state. Poaching escalated as a result, both because people no longer had a stake in preserving wildlife and because the local people took what they saw as rightfully theirs. Relations between wildlife officers and local people were increasingly strained as government officials attempted to enforce the law amid declining wildlife populations. The Lupande Development project resulted from the need to develop a management strategy that would reconcile local needs with improved wildlife management and conservation. The project included establishing various wildlife management committees who began planning for the use of wildlife as resources; training and employing local villagers as scouts to protect wildlife in the community; giving examples of sustained wildlife use; and sharing revenue from concession and trophy fees, which could be used to finance local community improvements.

Between 1984 and 1987 poaching levels declined by 90 percent, the wildlife population increased, and local residents benefited from access to game meat and wildlife-related employment. The Administrative Design for Game Management Areas (ADMADE) project was developed to extend the success of the Lupande project into other game management areas. More than 400 village scouts have been trained and employed under ADMADE. Revenues from hunting concessions alone have returned over $230,000 to local communities for development projects. In 1990 the government of Zambia agreed to divide the revenue from trophy and license fees—previously paid to the central treasury—between the central government and communities in the ADMADE program. This may effectively double community revenues. The portion of the funds received by the central government supports park management (15 percent) and the national tourist board (10 percent). Forty percent goes to wildlife management, including village scouts, and 35 percent goes directly to community projects.

Luangwa Integrated Rural Development Project (LIRDP), Zambia. LIRDP has the same roots as the Lupande development project and ADMADE. While

Lupande and ADMADE focus specifically on wildlife, LIRDP is a broader economic development program. Included in this program are agricultural improvement, nurseries, fisheries, wildlife resources, and infrastructure development, particularly road construction. The program is also coordinating credit for villagers, provision of agricultural inputs, and marketing systems. Apart from the substantial external funding from donors, most of the funds for LIRDP are derived from wildlife revenues; however, the allocation of revenues from wildlife use differs substantially from ADMADE's. Sixty percent of LIRDP revenues go to project management costs such as village scouts and road construction, and the remainder goes to community projects.

Nazinga Game Ranch, Burkina Faso. The ranch was conceived to protect and conserve wildlife through game meat production. The ranch has been extremely successful in restoring (principally through dam construction and fire control) and managing the formerly degraded habitat and in mounting antipoaching operations. This has re-

sulted in dramatic increases in the populations of large mammals found on the ranch. Economic studies have suggested that game ranching at Nazinga can be profitable, although game meat production has not yet resulted in any direct economic benefits to the local population. Local participation in revenues from meat production and from tourism have been planned but not implemented. Hundreds of local people were employed by the project during its construction phase.

Surprisingly, the single greatest benefit realized by the local population has been a substantial increase in fishing opportunities. The creation of numerous permanent water points about the ranch has greatly increased fish populations. The ranch has implemented a fisheries management program to control and regulate access to fishing rights. Permits are issued free for subsistence fishing or specially authorized groups such as a women's cooperative, and for a fee to groups who wish to fish commercially. (For a more detailed treatment of the wildlife component of natural resource management, see Kiss 1990.)

6. *Local participation*

While the overall goal of integrated conservation-development projects (ICDPs) is to conserve biological diversity, specific project activities are focused on people and on changing human behavior. Not surprisingly, therefore, nearly all of the planning documents for the case study projects emphasize local participation. Few of the projects, however, have specified what they mean by participation, nor detailed how they expect local participation in project development activities to reduce threats to nearby protected areas. Some uncertainty and ambiguity thus surround the issue of local participation in ICDPs, in theory and in practice.

This chapter addresses local participation—in development generally and in ICDPs specifically—asking *what* local people are participating in, *who* is participating, and *how* they get to participate. The chapter also describes the efforts by the case study projects to elicit local participation and examines the implications for protected area management.

Concern with community participation in development projects is not new (Midgeley 1986). Its importance was highlighted in the World Bank's 1975 sectoral policy paper on rural development, although evaluations of subsequent failed rural development projects lamented its absence (see chapter 4). Although unambiguous examples of successful participation are rare, local participation has recently become virtually indispensable in discussions of development. Failure to emphasize participation dramatically increases the chance of rejection for proposed development efforts. Despite the popularity of participation, Cernea (1985), among others, has argued that local participation is still more myth than reality in rural development programs. The organizations implementing ICDPs are thus attempting to implement a concept that the development community itself has found elusive.

What does local participation mean?

Chapter 5 described examples of social and economic benefits for local people that resulted from ICDP activities. Is this local participation? Most likely not. Local participation viewed as a *process* goes well beyond simply sharing in social and economic benefits. Local participation has been described as "empowering people to mobilize their own capacities, be social actors rather than passive subjects, manage the resources, make decisions, and control the activities that affect their lives" (Cernea 1985, 10).

Projects may be classified on the basis of their approaches to and relationships with the intended beneficiaries. At one end are projects that perceive local peoples' involvement as passive—the *beneficiary* approach. The goals of this approach to development are tangible economic benefits, although those who are to receive them have only a limited role in generating them. At the other end are projects that seek to involve people in the process of their own development, adopting a *participatory* approach. In these projects, development is perceived as a way to empower people and improve their ability to control their lives and use and manage resources. The project is a catalyst to stimulate self-reliance among the poor and underprivileged. This approach emphasizes the role of local institutions—both formal and informal—in providing people with the means to control their lives.

Projects with a beneficiary orientation generally set their goals in terms of changes in readily measurable indexes, such as income levels, farm productivity, infant mortality rates, and literacy rates. Project success is then gauged by improvements in these indexes. The goals and measures of effectiveness in projects with a participatory orientation are more elusive. Eventually such projects seek to achieve goals similar to those of beneficiary projects; however, they are oriented more toward establishing a process leading to change that can be sustained after the project ends.

Paul (1987) summarizes much of the literature on the participatory approach by suggesting that its objectives include increasing project effectiveness, increasing the capacity of beneficiaries to take responsibility for project activities, and facilitating cost sharing through local contributions of land, money, or labor. Others have pointed to the importance of involving stakeholders—intended beneficiaries—to give them a vested interest in, and presumably greater commitment to, achieving project goals. It is not easy to measure achievements against these kinds of objectives, particularly over short periods, while projects are still under way and before more tangible benefits have become apparent.

It is difficult to classify the case studies according to participatory or beneficiary approach, for several reasons. First, some projects encouraged participation in some components and activities but not in others. Second, the ability or willingness of local people to participate in projects varies significantly even at a single site. Third, participation implies at least some recognition of empowerment through a democratic process. As is the case with rural development in general, many of the communities where ICDPs are operating are rigidly hierarchical, with strong local leaders. In these circumstances the opportunities for participation among disadvantaged groups, such as women, the landless, and ethnic minorities, may be limited.

Despite these caveats, projects in three of the case study areas can be said to have adopted a consistently participatory approach. The projects in Annapurna (Nepal), Khao Yai (Thailand), and Osa Peninsula (Costa Rica) each started with a clearly stated goal of eliciting local participation, and commitment to a process of participation was clearly reflected in the activity choices. Three other case study projects involved local people in consultation before protected areas were established—Amboseli (Kenya), Beza Mahafaly (Madagascar), and Sian Ka'an (Mexico). The remaining projects adopted a more-or-less beneficiary approach.

Forms of participation

The literature (especially Cohen and Uphoff 1977; Paul 1987; and Salmen 1987) identifies five main areas in which local people can participate in rural development projects:

- *Information-gathering*. Project designers or managers both collect information from and share information with intended beneficiaries on the overall project concept and goals.
- *Consultation*. Intended beneficiaries are consulted on key issues during the project. Beneficiaries have an opportunity to interact and provide feedback during project design, implementation, or both.
- *Decisionmaking*. Beneficiaries participate in decisionmaking for project design or implementation, implying a greater degree of control and responsibility than the passive acceptance of possibly-unwanted benefits.
- *Initiating action*. When beneficiary groups identify a new need in a project and decide to respond to it, they are taking the initiative for their own development. This is different from acting or deciding on tasks or issues identified by the project.
- *Evaluation*. Participatory evaluation by beneficiaries can provide valuable insights and lessons for project design and implementation—information that otherwise is likely to remain unknown.

These areas seem as applicable to ICDPs as to rural development projects. They are not necessarily cumulative or sequential. For example, there can be local decisionmaking without prior participation in information-gathering or in consultation. A project may not have a consistent approach to participation that stretches across all of its components or activities. To use Paul's (1987) term, project components may each have their own "intensity" of participation. However, despite this potential for variability in approaches to participation, most of the case study projects made implicit choices early in the project about the relative emphasis they planned to give to local participation (box 6.1).

Local participation in projects as defined for this study implies the consistent involvement of local people in strategic project issues rather than their occasional or limited involvement in day-to-day activities. By this measure, local participation was substantially incorporated in *information-gathering* in Amboseli (Kenya), Annapurna (Nepal), Boscosa (Costa Rica), Khao Yai (Thailand), and Sian Ka'an (Mexico); in *consultation* in the same projects plus Beza Mahafaly (Madagascar) and Lupande/ADMADE (Zambia); in *decisionmaking* in Annapurna (Nepal), Beza Mahafaly (Madagascar), Boscosa (Costa Rica), Lupande/ADMADE (Zambia),

---

Box 6.1 Effective local participation

Annapurna, Nepal. Prior to the project, a three-member survey team (two Nepalese and one expatriate) spent six months collecting information in the area that eventually became the multiple-use Annapurna Conservation Area. The team developed a provisional project design and management plan based on discussions with leaders and villagers throughout the region. After the survey, however, the team concluded that a national park designation along traditional restrictive lines would not be well received. After considering various options, they recommended a new legal designation, a conservation area that would specifically allow hunting, collection of forest products, allocation of visitor fees for local development, and delegation of management authority to the village level. Extensive consultations and local participation in decisionmaking have continued to be a feature of the project, and the project managers have, wherever possible, resisted the unilateral imposition of regulations affecting local people.

At the outset the project recognized the need to establish the trust of a skeptical local population, to convince them that they would benefit from—or at least not be harmed by—the project. The second step was to attempt to motivate people to make resource-management decisions. In any community activities, the project has avoided free gifts and always insisted on local participation, with cash or labor. At least a 50 percent local contribution is usually targeted and, wherever possible, inputs by the project are limited to contributions in kind (purchased goods).

Khao Yai, Thailand. Before beginning the project at Sup Tai village, the Research and Evaluation Division of the Population and Development Association of Thailand, one of the implementing nongovernmental organizations conducted an extensive baseline survey. The survey revealed that the inhabitants of Sup Tai were poorer than the average for Thailand. About 80 percent of the households were in debt, health and sanitation levels were low, and malaria was common. There were no formal village institutions capable of coordinating project activities. Literacy was low and one-third of the villagers, mostly recent immigrants, were without legal land title. The survey emphasized the extent to which the welfare of the villagers was linked to and dependent upon middlemen, from whom they received credit at 5 percent a month. It was apparent that the park provided an illegal source of income for many villagers. This survey had considerable influence on the project design. Two subsequent surveys have measured progress against these baseline results. All of the surveys included numerous interviews with villagers.

Osa Peninsula, Costa Rica. The Boscosa project developed and employed what project papers termed a "participative communal extension process," which emphasizes community involvement in project design, execution, and evaluation. For example, in one pilot community, land tenure, land use, land-use capability, and current agricultural practices were evaluated. Farmers were interviewed to determine their experiences with, and desire for, alternative crops or techniques. With help from the project, twenty-three farmers formed a production association. With technical assistance from the project, the association decided on crops and developed a communal nursery. Following this early involvement in project design and decisionmaking, the community organized other initiatives such as agroforestry, reforestation with native species, a women's arts and crafts group, and primary timber processing using a portable saw. A recent internal evaluation of the project concludes that the community "shows a more conscious approach toward forest productive management and has a long-term planning outlook on aspects such as resource use, development of proposals for new initiatives, buying of "forestry permits," and development of a community-managed forest. The Boscosa project has actively contributed to encouraging and sponsoring forums for dialogue about conservation and development on the peninsula by numerous interest groups, including small farmers, loggers, gold miners, and tourism proponents. The project has also provided technical support, especially in organizational development, to local organizations in the region.

---

and in the Yanesha Forestry component of Central Selva (Peru); in *initiating action* in the Boscosa (Costa Rica) project; and in *evaluation* in the Khao Yai (Thailand) project at Sup Tai. While some of the other projects featured occasional or limited participation, it did not appear to be a consistent or principal emphasis.

How do projects promote participation?

Two principal approaches to organizing and sustaining community participation in projects can be identified from the literature: employing agents of change and building local institutions. Agents of change are also referred to as field workers, extension workers, community organizers, or animators. Paul (1987) distinguishes two categories: field workers employed by the agency implement-

ing the project, and workers or volunteers from among the beneficiaries who act as community mobilizers.

Agents of change

Ideally, agents of change do not act as leaders and do not tell the community what to do (Midgley 1986; Tilakaratna 1987). Their task is to foster grassroots participation and build local institutions. Several case study ICDPs employed agents of change (box 6.2).

Most of the field staff of the case study projects have essentially acted as agents of change. In most cases these people, whether expatriates or nationals, were experienced, well-trained, energetic, and knowledgeable. Trusting relationships frequently have been developed with local people and their

---

Box 6.2 Agents of change

Air-Tenere, Niger. The project has established a network of village representatives from among the pastoralists. The selected representatives are people recognized locally as having authority within their herding groups. Their tasks are to be well-informed about the rules, goals, and activities in the reserve; to encourage others to support these rules and goals; and to inform enforcement authorities of any infractions of the rules observed within their districts. These representatives receive no remuneration from the project, although they attend an annual workshop sponsored by the project.

East Usambara, Tanzania. The area selected for the initial project focus contained about 25,000 people, many of them living two days' travel time from the project headquarters. To promote interaction with these communities, the project selected a village coordinator from each of fifteen target villages. The regional government pays the village coordinator's salaries and has guaranteed to maintain the positions permanently. The village coordinators are the primary link between the project and the villages, meeting monthly as a group to report progress and problems. They are either trained by the project or sent to attend short courses. The village coordinators have begun working closely with farmers in their own villages, and most have established agricultural demonstration plots.

Khao Yai, Thailand. At Sup Tai village, the principal agent of change is the full-time project manager from the Population and Development Association, the implementing nongovernmental organization. This manager has hired a small number of local staff but works directly with villagers on project activities. The Population and Development Association has been active in thousands of villages throughout Thailand and its field personnel are well educated and trained, with extensive community development experience.

South Luangwa, Zambia. The main local agents of change are the village scouts. These are young men—selected by local chiefs—who are employed by the National Park and Wildlife Service and trained in wildlife enforcement. Hiring game scouts from local villages has been an effective way of generating community support for reducing poaching. The next stage of the project calls for hiring some fifty community facilitators to monitor socioeconomic effects and to involve more disadvantaged members of the community, especially women.

Talamanca, Costa Rica. The project began a community technicians program in 1989 with representatives from each of forty communities where nurseries have been established. The program is intended to develop local leaders who can provide information on agricultural and agroforestry development and can act as liaisons between their community and outside agencies. Each community selects a representative, plus an alternate, to receive advanced training in agriculture and agroforestry. Representatives tend to be younger, better-educated members of the community. When they return to their villages, they train others in what they have learned, often on an individual basis. Farmers work on the community technicians' land in exchange for the time they receive from the community technician.

---

leaders, many of whom had been suspicious and distrustful, if not openly hostile, when the projects began. Project staff frequently have appeared to personify the projects from the local perspective, and their leadership and counsel obviously have been valued in many of the targeted communities. Not surprisingly, there were several examples among the case studies where it was difficult to imagine project activities continuing without these individuals. In other words, care must be taken to avoid creating new dependencies.

Institution building

It has been argued that participation through institutions or organizations is more likely to be effective and sustained than individual participation (for example, Uphoff 1987). Local institutions can act as a focus of mobilization among local people and as a link between local people and external organizations, whether governmental or nongovernmental organization. Institution building has been defined by Midgeley (1986) as "the creation of procedures for democratic decision making at the local level and the involvement of

local people in these procedures to the extent that they [come to] regard them as the normal way of conducting community affairs." Several of the projects sought to build local institutions (box 6.3). Most of these institutions are of relatively recent origin and few, if any, have become independent of the projects.

Local participation issues for projects

Some ICDP managers recognize that building the capacity for people to make their own decisions and take initiative can be a long-term prospect. The need for patience can conflict with feelings of urgency about the need to change or stop destructive patterns of protected area degradation. This dilemma has been clearly expressed by the principal adviser to the Air-Tenere project in Niger:

> The intention is to involve local people in the design of projects.... However, while local communities may identify the problems which concern them (and which may or may not match the objectives of various projects or donors), true participation is often only

---

Box 6.3 Institution building

Annapurna, Nepal. The project promoted the establishment of a forest management committee in one village and lodge management committees in some of the villages along popular trekking routes. The forest management committee has helped reestablish community control over local forests, as existed prior to nationalization in the 1950s. Both the lodge and forest management committees have started to make some key resource management decisions, with prompting and support from the projects, although they are not yet close to becoming self-sufficient organizations.

Central Selva, Peru. The Amuesha Indians formed a six-person committee to determine the best structure for organizing forestry activities. The committee consisted of one representative from each of five communities and the proposed forestry activities administrator. A cooperative structure, similar to Amuesha communal government systems, was selected and, shortly thereafter, members from the five communities joined to establish a forestry cooperative. Members participate in working groups; the heads of working groups make decisions collectively. Although the members like the cooperative decisionmaking, not all of the native communities have joined the cooperative. This may be partly because the cooperative has not yet been able to generate revenue for participating communities, and because of the long distance between cooperative headquarters and some of the nonparticipating communities.

Khao Yai, Thailand. Project development and conservation activities at each village are centered around the environmental protection society. These institutions were created to enable villagers to take control of resource management and to encourage them to take some responsibility for safeguarding the national park. Considerable emphasis has been placed on establishing the credibility of the environmental protection society as a viable organization separate from the project centers. Low-interest loans funneled through the environmental protection society are the major incentive for villagers to participate. The training of elected environmental protection society committee members, particularly in the administration of loans, has advanced at one village but remains at an early stage elsewhere. A 1989 evaluation of the project saw little prospect of the committee members being able to take over the societies in the near future.

Lupande/ADMADE, Zambia. The administrative structure of Lupande/ADMADE was designed to balance national-level management with systems of local participation. The most decentralized unit is the Wildlife Management Subauthority, with one subauthority for each chiefdom. Members of each subauthority include the chief and headmen, head teachers, party chairmen, and other local authorities. One responsibility is to determine what community development projects will be funded with revenue returned from wildlife use. However, these groups are not yet free-standing local institutions; they are closely tied into the national political system.

Osa Peninsula, Costa Rica. The Boscosa project has helped establish or strengthen numerous small, local organizations throughout the Osa Peninsula. These organizations include a locally organized cooperative whose ultimate objective is to process wood into low-priced furniture, and agricultural producers' associations in three different communities. The project has also tried to strengthen existing community groups. Project staff have trained local communities in program development, proposal writing, and fund-raising. At least fourteen proposals have been submitted by communities for agroforestry, reforestation, forest-products processing, and other activities. Several have already received funding and others are being reviewed by a variety of donors. Most of these institutions have been established recently; none yet has shown the capacity to assume responsibility for local resource management.

Talamanca, Costa Rica. The project helped create the Talamanca Association of Small Producers (APPTA), a regional procurement, processing, and marketing association. The association was established in 1987 and is administered locally by farmers involved in the project. It is one of the few regional outlets for procurement of agricultural inputs or marketing assistance. APPTA has not yet been involved in marketing local products, but it has established a store where it is selling agricultural inputs. APPTA has also completed feasibility studies on marketing and processing major agricultural crops in the region. APPTA is now independent of the project, although it maintains close ties.

User groups have been established for community nurseries and women's organic-farming groups. About 600 households in forty communities have decided to participate. Each group decides how to organize the work, what seedlings to establish, the labor contributions from members, and so on. While these user groups are not formal institutions, they are often the only organized groups in the communities.

---

developed after a project has already been accepted and is under implementation.... The urgency of the region's conservation problems dictates against the lengthy process of developing local support and participatory capacity, however important this may be for long-term success.... The project's philosophy is that popular support and, eventually, voluntary and internally motivated participation, can only be achieved through a belief in what one is doing. Therefore, the approach which the project is taking is to pro-

duce tangible evidence of the beneficial results of its various activities. (Newby 1989, quoted in Kiss 1990, 57)

Some barriers to local participation are common to any development project, including ICDPs. As mentioned above, existing authority structures in many societies inhibit widespread participation in decisionmaking. In addition, national governments may limit the extent of local empowerment, particularly where they perceive a threat to their own authority.

Overlooked by most of the projects is the fact that ICDPs by definition limit participation. For an ICDP to achieve its basic objective—biodiversity conservation—people can only be empowered in aspects of development, including local resource management, that do not lead to overexploitation or degradation of the protected wildlife and wildlands. In practice this can be very difficult to achieve using economic incentives. There is always likely to be a conflict of interest between rural people's ability to earn a living and the management of nearby protected areas. It is unrealistic to assume that resource-poor people, living next to what may appear to them to be limitless resources of land, trees, plants, and animals, will readily support park conservation ideals. ICDPs are based on the principles of mitigating such conflicts of interest by promoting alternative income sources and education programs. But the conflicts cannot be expected to disappear, and the general need for strict enforcement appears inescapable.

Modified local participation

Although all of the case study projects are committed to participation in principle, most have treated local people as passive beneficiaries of project activities and have failed to involve people in the process of change and their own development. As a result, the targets of the projects often have no stake in or commitment to the activities being promoted. None of the projects based on this beneficiary approach has demonstrated significant progress toward its goals.

On the other hand, some of the projects adopting a participatory approach have made important progress in winning the trust and confidence of skeptical local populations and eliciting the participation of community members in project-initiated activities. Locally credible networks of agents of change and new institutions consistent with the ICDP goals have been established at several sites, but only one has yet demonstrated the capacity to operate independently of the project or to have a significant impact on nearby parks. Tangible progress is thus difficult to demonstrate.

This apparent lack of progress is at least partly attributable to the projects' relatively short duration and illustrates how lengthy and difficult a process eliciting local participation in any development project can be. The limited experience to date suggests that at least a decade is likely to be needed—instead of one or two years. Such lengthy periods will require patience and commitment from donors, ICDP managers, and the intended beneficiaries. These long periods are also likely to be accompanied by a continued escalation of threats against the protected area that the project is trying to conserve.

Neither the beneficiary nor the participatory approach to ICDPs has been demonstrably effective so far in achieving ICDP goals in the case study projects. The beneficiary approach may not be sustainable, and the participatory approach takes long to implement. Although neither approach can substitute for enforcement, participation can facilitate a more cooperative relationship between protected areas and local people and thus make enforcement more humane and acceptable.

A balanced approach would seem essential. In the long term, local participation, as defined in this section, should be sought as much as possible. However, short-term benefits also are needed to establish the projects' credibility locally and to overcome distrust among the target population. The continuing—and probably intensified—need for enforcement will have to be balanced between these long- and short-term goals. The appropriate nature of this balance for individual projects will, once again, depend on a thorough assessment of local social, political, economic, cultural, and biological factors.

7. Participating organizations

There are three principal roles for organizations in an integrated conservation-development project (ICDP):

- *Project implementation.* The case study projects were executed by a mix of government agencies and nongovernmental organizations, independently or in partnership. Some of the government agencies were those specifically responsible for protected area management, but others were not. The nongovernmental organizations ranged from large, sophisticated international conservation groups to small local organizations for which the ICDP represented a major undertaking.
- *Management of the protected area.* Personnel of the government agencies managing the parks played various roles in the ICDPs. Managers of the traditional parks generally had little or no direct involvement in project management. Some were highly skeptical of the ICDP's intentions; their collaboration with the project, if any, tended to be unenthusiastic and weighted down by bureaucratic procedures. At multiple-use sites, the management agencies tended to be much more involved with the projects, either collaborating fully with the project implementation organization or actually managing the project.
- *Source of funds.* Financing was generally provided by international conservation nongovernmental organizations, by international development agencies, and—less frequently—by national governments and by multiple donors. World Bank loans funded the Amboseli (Kenya) and Dumoga-Bone (Indonesia) projects and USAID grants supported the Andohahela and Beza Mahafaly (Madagascar), Bururi (Burundi), Central Selva (Peru), Khao Yai (TEAM) (Thailand), and South Luangwa (Zambia) projects. The World Wildlife Fund-U.S. participated in funding or implementing all, or portions, of the Andohahela and Beza Mahafaly (Madagascar), Annapurna (Nepal), Boscosa and Talamanca (Costa Rica), Central Selva (Peru), Mon-

arch and Sian Ka'an (Mexico), and South Luangwa, Zambia projects.

Some interesting arrangements and partnerships emerged from the case studies. For example:

- The project at Khao Yai National Park, Thailand, started as a result of collaboration between a large Thai nongovernmental organization with extensive rural development experience and a small recently formed national conservation nongovernmental organization interested primarily in wildlife protection. Government participation was minimal.
- The government of Nepal delegated its management authority over the Annapurna Conservation Area to a national conservation nongovernmental organization.
- No national nongovernmental organizations are involved in the African case studies—all of the participating nongovernmental organizations are foreign-based. The Air-Tenere, Volcanoes, and Usambara projects are being executed by the governments of Niger, Rwanda, and Tanzania respectively, with substantial technical assistance—and funding at Air-Tenere—from international conservation nongovernmental organizations.
- In Latin America most of the projects are being implemented by nongovernmental organizations with little direct government participation. But authorizations and cooperation were frequently required from a bewilderingly complex assortment of ministries, departments, and agencies of the national and local governments.

This chapter discusses the roles of different organizations in the case study projects, identifying the strengths and weaknesses of the participating government agencies, the nongovernmental organizations, and the donors (or lenders). The chapter then discusses which organizations ought to be involved in ICDPs, and in what capacity.

Government agencies

Protected area management agencies are generally found in the ministries responsible for forests (Asia and Latin America) or wildlife (Africa). Their challenging mandate—managing large areas of land for conservation—is frequently out of all proportion to their minuscule resources, inadequate legal powers, and lack of political influence. Consequently, these agencies tend to appear ineffectual in managing and protecting their parks.

Outside park boundaries the situation is worse. Park managers tend to be poorly placed to address the problems confronting local people. Few park management agencies have jurisdiction outside park boundaries, and the legal authority over lands adjacent to parks is usually shared between local government and several ministries. Most of the agencies lack equipment and the most basic technical expertise. Field staff are often poorly paid, ill-equipped, ill-trained, lacking opportunities for advancement, and isolated from their families for long periods. In combination with the traditional orientation toward an enforcement role, these constraints ensure that most park management agencies lack the inclination or capacity to respond constructively to local people-park issues. Not surprisingly, this has led to conflicts of interest between park managers and local communities, leading to resentment, hardship, and sometimes violence.

One of the earliest and most widely reported examples of cooperation between government officials and local people is at Royal Chitwan National Park in Nepal. This arrangement has provided what appears to be only temporary relief, however, and continued strict enforcement may be the only hope for Chitwan (box 7.1).

Despite these constraints, government agencies have played important roles in ICDPs either through direct participation—by taking a lead role in implementing the project—or through indirect participation by delegating their authority or facilitating project performance. Beyond the immediate project context, the effectiveness of government programs in providing basic services to rural communities—such as education, health care, and road maintenance—are also key factors in determining income levels and living standards in communities near parks, thereby affecting the pressure likely to be exerted on park resources.

Direct participation

Government agencies have taken lead roles in the projects at Air-Tenere, (Niger, box 7.2), Amboseli (Kenya), Andohahela (Madagascar), Bururi (Burundi), Chitwan (Nepal), Dumoga-Bone (Indonesia), South Luangwa (Zambia), and Volcanoes (Rwanda). In some of these projects, nongovernmental organizations working in international conservation such as African Wildlife Foundation, Wildlife Conservation International, International Union for Conservation of Nature and Natural Resources (IUCN), and World Wildlife Fund have provided extensive technical assistance and much of the total funding. (Chapter 3 describes the structure of the Usambara project.)

In cases where government agencies have taken a lead role, financial sustainability after the project ends has sometimes been uncertain. The Amboseli, Kenya, and Bururi, Burundi, projects encountered substantial problems after external project funding was exhausted, leading to significant breakdowns in project operations. In Tanzania, regional and national government agencies have allocated considerable staff resources to the Usambara project and are committed to creating permanent positions for the fifteen village coordinators hired locally and trained by the project. Nonetheless, the project still may be threatened by discontinuity of external funding. In Zambia, there are enough safari revenues to support the project, but the international ivory ban could cause major revenue shortfalls for the government agency.

Governments may not always share the conservation priority of ICDP staff, particularly when tour-

---

Box 7.1 Grass collection in Royal Chitwan National Park, Nepal

Prior to the park's establishment in 1973, local people had used the area to collect fuelwood, graze livestock, and collect tall grasses for building material. For two years after the establishment of the park, these activities were banned. Several hundred soldiers from the Royal Nepal Army were deployed to enforce the regulations, resulting in frequent conflicts and arrests. The local population is rapidly expanding, and the pressure on land and resources appears to be such that local people have little choice but to collect fuelwood illegally and to take their cattle into the park for grazing. Chitwan appears only to have bought some time, because the conflict will increase with the disappearance of the few remaining patches of forest outside the national park that have satisfied local needs for fuelwood and grazing land. Without the continuing presence of the army, it seems inevitable that Chitwan would have been lost as a park several years ago.

Box 7.2 Organizational structure of the Air-Tenere project, Niger

The project is administered by the Service of Wildlife and Fisheries of the Ministry of Agriculture and Environment. The on-site project director, a Niger forester, is directly responsible to the director of wildlife and fisheries in Niamey. He is aided in his administrative duties by the assistant director, also a Niger forester. Other Niger nationals on the project staff include three foresters, three guides, four nurserymen, four extension workers, two site foremen, and a garage staff of eight, including drivers. Expatriate participants include the IUCN/World Wildlife Fund representative based in Niamey, who is the principal project coordinator-adviser, an adviser for conservation, an adviser for rural development, a head mechanic (a German volunteer), and two biologists (Peace Corps volunteers).

---

ism revenues are at stake. In Rwanda, the Volcanoes project is financially self-sustaining because of the high revenues derived from foreign tourists viewing the gorillas. However, the government is exerting considerable pressure to increase the scale of tourism and thus generate more foreign-currency earnings. Conservation interests are concerned that increased contact could have a detrimental effect on gorillas.

Indirect participation

In a few cases, government authority over protected areas has been delegated to a nongovernmental organization. The Nepal government has relinquished most of its authority over the multiple-use Annapurna Conservation Area to the King Mahendra Trust for Nature Conservation, a national nongovernmental organization, while the University of Madagascar has been given jurisdiction over the Beza Mahafaly Reserve. Monarca, A.C. has an agreement with the Mexican government to provide education, trail maintenance, guards, and so on, at one of the Monarch Butterfly Overwintering Reserves, but relations and collaboration are often strained. There were no other examples of effective collaboration between national nongovernmental organizations and their governments among the case study projects.

Governments can also facilitate, authorize, or at least tolerate projects without actively participating. One of the most important ways for gov-

ernments to help ICDPs is the passage of legislation to establish multiple-use areas (as in Nepal and in Niger) or to clarify jurisdiction outside the boundaries of existing protected areas (as is being considered in Indonesia and in Nepal)(chapter 2).

At times governments indirectly hinder ICDPs. As discussed above, in the absence of specific enabling legislation, most agencies have lacked the jurisdiction needed to take the lead in the case study ICDPs, even in the unusual circumstances where they have had the capability and adequate resources. As a result, to work in communities outside parks, some projects have had to consult and work with complex and frequently overlapping local and national government agencies (box 7.3). Projects with activities in different sectors (for example, agriculture, tourism, forestry, education, and health) often have had to reach agreement with several government agencies. This task has proved to be a considerable burden for the projects in Latin America.

The Dumoga-Bone project in Indonesia placed considerable emphasis on incorporating the views of the many local and national government agencies that had an interest in the irrigation projects, the transmigration of farmers, and the establishment of a national park. Frequent on-site meetings with these agencies contributed to the timely resolution of differences and helped to prevent bureaucratic procedures from unduly delaying the project. However, this was a $60 million project involving 8,000 farmers. Smaller projects with less

---

Box 7.3 Complexities of governmental relations at Talamanca, Costa Rica

ANAI, the small local nongovernmental organization executing the Talamanca project in Costa Rica, has limited staff resources. The organization has agreements with, and receives funds from, several government ministries, including those for natural resources, justice, and agriculture. For a land-titling project component, ANAI has worked with additional public and private agencies. The project area includes several different categories of protected area—including a biosphere reserve, a wildlife refuge, Indian reservations, and a national park. Separate government offices administer each of these. In addition to these four agencies, ANAI must coordinate its activities with at least ten more government agencies. The elections in 1990 necessitated the building of a completely new set of relationships with incoming personnel in each government agency.

---

obvious economic significance may not be able to attract this level of cooperation.

In many countries where protected areas are under pressure, there is little prospect—at least in the short term—of management agencies making a meaningful contribution to ICDPs, even with funding and technical assistance from international organizations. The Administrative Design for Game Management Areas (ADMADE) program in Zambia is an exception, although the success of this program may be closely related to the specific set of conditions associated with wildlife safari hunting in game management areas outside national parks in southern African savannas (see also Kiss 1990).

Strengthening protected area management agencies to enable them to manage protected areas adequately would require long-term investments in expanding park and reserve networks, establishing conservation monitoring programs, training field staff and their managers, purchasing and maintaining equipment, and improving salaries, working conditions, and career prospects to attract more and better educated employees. These agencies also require support to increase their capacity to absorb funds from foreign lenders and donors and to coordinate their responses to the diverse interests and priorities of these organizations.

Finally, and of critical importance in the ICDP context, these agencies need to change from a purely enforcement orientation to one substantially more sympathetic to communities living in and around parks. This will require not only changes in attitude at all agency levels but also completely new skills in such areas as communication, extension, education, and mediation.

Nongovernmental organizations

As several authors have pointed out (for example, Brown and Korten 1989), the term nongovernmental organization (NGO) embraces such a diverse range of organizations that its value as a classifica-tion is limited. The World Bank describes NGO as "private organizations that pursue activities to relieve suffering, promote the interests of the poor, protect the environment or undertake community development" (Cernea 1988b, 43).

Role in the case study projects

A few principal categories of NGOs have been encountered in this study, with the most basic distinction being between national and international ones. The national NGOs tend to be either development- or conservation-oriented, but not both. The only national organization with extensive development experience in the sample was the Population and Community Development Association (Thailand). National NGOs played principal roles in the projects at Annapurna (Nepal), Khao Yai (Thailand), Monarch (Mexico), and Talamanca (Costa Rica). The organizations were rarely involved in protected area enforcement, tending to place greater emphasis on local development and education.

Some of the national NGOs are truly "national," with extensive resources and considerable expertise gained through project experience. These include the King Mahendra Trust for Nature Conservation in Nepal (box 7.4) and the Population and Development Association in Thailand. The other national NGOs involved in projects in Latin America are much smaller. ANAI (in the Talamanca project in Costa Rica) and Friends of Sian Ka'an and Monarca, A.C. (both in Mexico) were established to conserve specific protected areas and their surrounds. In each of these cases, there is little distinction between the activities of the project and those of the NGO.

Most of the international NGOs represented in the case studies are widely known and well-established conservation organizations, including Wildlife Conservation International (part of the New York Zoological Society), IUCN, and World Wildlife Fund. An exception has been Catholic Relief Ser-

---

Box 7.4 The King Mahendra Trust for Nature Conservation, Nepal

Established in 1982, the King Mahendra Trust for Nature Conservation is the largest and most influential conservation organization in Nepal. Royal patronage has contributed significantly to the trust's success. The King Mahendra Trust also has close ties to influential politicians and has been given a remarkably autonomous and significant role in the management of the Annapurna Conservation Area. This is probably a unique arrangement for an NGO in Asia—or for any NGO on an issue of such global importance. The trust may raise money directly from overseas and has been able to lobby successfully for new legislation needed to guarantee its autonomy. The trust has been able to bypass many of the inefficiencies and time-consuming procedures associated with government agencies and to execute projects with a relatively slim and flexible bureaucracy.

vices, an international development NGO participating in the Burundi projects and the Conservation Foundation/World Wildlife Fund, which was directly involved in implementation of the Boscosa project. No other international development NGOs have participated, although a small number, particularly CARE, have recently started to become involved in ICDPS. International NGOs have seldom been involved directly in project implementation, tending instead to work with government agencies or local NGOs. The international organizations' principal role has been to contribute or raise funds and to provide expatriate technical assistance, sometimes in the form of the project manager or leader.

There was an intriguing partnership between two national NGOs, the Population and Development Association of Thailand, and Wildlife Fund Thailand, at Khao Yai, Thailand (chapter 3 and box 7.5). This partnership combined the Population and Development Association's extensive project management and participatory rural development experience with Wildlife Fund Thailand's conservation expertise and knowledge of wildlife issues. The two organizations' capacities appeared to complement each other. Unfortunately, this partnership did not survive more than a few years, after which the two NGOs each began concentrating their efforts in separate communities on the park boundaries. Problems facing each of the organizations in implementing their now-separate projects can, to some extent, be attributed to the loss of the balanced approach that had been facilitated by the partnership.

Strengths and weaknesses

Conservation-oriented NGOs have taken a leading role in the first generation of ICDPS. The conservation groups have previously proved effective in highlighting environmental issues and concerns, devising education and awareness programs, and lobbying governments and international agencies. Conservation NGOs have also made substantial contributions to establishing and managing protected areas by mobilizing funds and providing expatriate technical assistance. However, groups having little experience in development have struggled to implement effective development within ICDPS.

On the other hand, development NGOs have implemented many small, low-cost, and innovative projects that have benefitted poor people in remote rural communities throughout the developing world. The NGO approach to development has been associated with sensitivity to local needs, flexibility, and site-specific solutions involving appropriate technologies. This bottom-up approach can help to avoid the cumbersome bureaucracies of central governments and the top-down blueprint designs of rural development projects sponsored by international development agencies (chapter 4). In ICDPS, however, many development NGOs have only recently started to introduce environmental components to their projects, and few have given explicit consideration to the conservation of biodiversity.

NGOs have played a valuable role in identifying and promoting innovative project concepts and drawing attention to the need for ICDPS. This role is particularly important because many of the responsible government agencies are unwilling or incapable of reacting. What, then, are the appropriate future ICDP roles for conservation and development NGOs?

A recent review of World Bank projects involving NGOs reported that many NGOs see their main role as serving as an institutional bridge between a project and its beneficiaries, linking project objectives and activities to the needs and environment of beneficiaries (Salmen and Eaves 1989). The

---

Box 7.5 Nongovernmental organizations in partnership at Khao Yai National Park, Thailand

Two NGOs—the Population and Community Development Association and Wildlife Fund Thailand—agreed to jointly develop and implement the pilot project. The Population and Development Association has been organizing community development activities since 1974 and is the largest NGO in Thailand. Its activities have reached more than 16,000 villages and have led to improvements in health, family planning, and income. Its approach is characterized by community participation in decisionmaking, training of villagers, and the provision of low-interest credit. Wildlife Fund Thailand was founded in 1983 and has rapidly achieved prominence by attracting attention to some of Thailand's most important environmental issues. It is affiliated with the World Wildlife Fund-International.

The Population and Development Association and Wildlife Fund Thailand started the project in 1985 at the village of Sup Tai. Although they now manage separate projects, the two organizations still collaborate. By 1989 their "development for conservation" programs had expanded to thirteen villages, ten of them managed by Wildlife Fund Thailand and three of them by Population and Development Associates. Wildlife Fund Thailand reached another forty villages with mobile conservation education units.

World Bank study argued that involvement of intermediary NGOs in Bank-sponsored projects can help to translate beneficiary needs and knowledge of local conditions to the World Bank or the borrower, translate project guidelines to communities, organize beneficiaries to take advantage of project benefits, deliver services to less accessible populations, and serve as intermediaries to other NGOs. These seem logical roles for NGOs in ICDPs.

In addition to their many strengths, however, NGOs also have limitations (box 7.6). Annis (1987), among others, has written that the strengths for which NGOs are acclaimed can also be serious weaknesses—that "small-scale" can merely mean "insignificant," "politically independent" can mean "powerless" or "disconnected," and "innovative" can mean simply "temporary" or "unsustainable." These potential weaknesses suggest a need for some caution in assessing the capacity of any NGO to execute ICDPs unassisted.

Promoting development has proved difficult even for NGOs experienced in managing rural development projects. Doing so for an ICDP would likely prove extremely challenging for international conservation NGOs with limited experience in projects targeting poor rural people or for national conservation or environmental NGOs that were originally established to lobby governments, raise money for the establishment of specific protected areas, or raise conservation awareness through education programs.

Another constraint facing NGOs is the resistance of some governments and their agencies to NGO involvement in development projects. Governments frequently feel threatened by the growth of NGOs and often react to their activities with suspicion and hostility (Cernea 1988b). Governments may regard some NGO activities as an unwelcome intrusion in politics. In turn, NGOs sometimes face the dilemma of accepting some government funds and putting their credibility or future autonomy at risk.

Finally, the reports and literature emanating from some of the NGOs sponsoring the projects suggest confusion between what has been planned and what has been achieved. In some cases the public relations effort has been set in motion too early. This has several undesirable effects: it suggests that the ICDP approach is relatively quick and easy, when in fact ICDPs are complex and long-term commitments; it overrates some weak projects, rather than concentrating on needed improvements; it places unrealistic expectations on some promising projects too early; it inhibits the experimentation and learning that are essential in such innovative ventures; and it can lead to large numbers of visitors, all requiring the valuable time of project managers.

Donors (and lenders)

Many donors have become increasingly interested in funding ICDPs as part of their expanding environmental mandates and growing interest in links between conservation and development. For the case study projects, principal funding sources have included multilateral organizations (the World Bank and the European Community), bilateral agencies (in Canada, the Netherlands, Norway, Sweden, Switzerland, the United States, and West Germany), private foundations, and the international NGOs (which, in turn, have their own funding sources, including private foundations).

Smaller national NGOs that are executing projects can spend considerable time on—and sometimes

---

Box 7.6 Strengths and weaknesses of nongovernmental organizations

Comparative advantages
- Reaching the rural poor, particularly in remote areas
- Facilitating local resource mobilization and promoting rural participation
- Delivering services at relatively low cost
- Finding innovative solutions

Comparative limitations
- Limited ability to scale-up successful projects
- Limited ability to develop community organizations that are self-sustaining after special staff and resources are withdrawn
- Lack of technical capacity for complex projects
- Lack of strategic perspective and linkages with other important actors
- Limited managerial and organizational capacities

Source: Brown and Korten (1989).

be overwhelmed by—requirements to write detailed proposals and evaluation reports and to meet regularly with donors. Examples include Amigos de Sian Ka'an, Mexico; ANAI's Talamanca project, Costa Rica; and Wildlife Fund Thailand's TEAM project at Khao Yai, Thailand. In some cases these tasks were overwhelming the modest administrative capacities of the organizations and detracting from the pressing daily management needs of the projects. Actual or perceived pressure from donors to report concrete results also resulted in some overoptimistic project analyses and internal evaluations. By contrast, most project field staff appeared realistic about the magnitude of the challenge they had taken on.

Many of the projects and donors have adopted time schedules that seem unrealistically short given their ambitious objectives. In particular, perhaps because they have been applying for short term grants, projects have tended to predict the achievement of financial self-sufficiency within a few years. Such predictions have proved unrealistic, particularly at sites where there are no alternative funding sources such as foreign tourists or safari hunters.

Some of the projects have been subject to alarming funding bottlenecks and have continued only through the remarkable persistence of their field staff. These include Andohahela and Beza Mahafaly (Madagascar), East Usambara (Tanzania), and TEAM at Khao Yai (Thailand). In some cases the delays were related to the renewal of short-term grants, while in others they were attributable to poor communications between the funding agency and the project.

The types of relationships between donors and case study projects vary considerably, but with notable exceptions, the donors tend to share a number of characteristics. Often they require that funds be expended rapidly over short periods, they require frequent reporting of tangible project achievements, they limit their financial commitments to two-to-three-year funding cycles, they have inefficient and overly bureaucratic mechanisms for transferring funds to field staff, and they invariably support "projects" instead of core activities of government agencies or NGOs. This study suggests that these characteristics reduce the likelihood of ICDPs being effective in achieving their goals.

Which organizations should be involved?

Reflecting the continuing debate over rural development project design, there is also an argument over whether ICDPs should follow a top-down or bottom-up approach (see, for example, Hough and Sherpa 1989). Top-down is associated with governments and with international organizations, and bottom-up is associated with NGOs. The case studies have revealed little convincing evidence that either governments or conservation or development NGOs, working independently, can effectively plan and implement ICDPs.

Government agencies interested in, or responsible for, conservation frequently lack financial resources and enough trained personnel, and are oriented away from community participation in natural resource management. It is thus difficult for them to execute ICDPs.

On the other hand, many projects implemented by NGOs have been tolerated rather than encouraged by government. Although this may result in projects that facilitate local decisionmaking, are sensitive to local community needs, and are independent of ponderous bureaucracies, there are three problems. First, conservation and development NGOs alone often lack the necessary expertise to identify, design, implement, or evaluate integrated projects. Second, NGO operations are unlikely to be permitted by most governments to reach a scale large enough to make a meaningful difference to the conservation of biological diversity. (The scale of the case study projects is considered in chapter 8.) Third, the prospects for project success are limited without the active participation of government in establishing a policy and legislative environment supportive of ICDPs. It could also be argued that without the basic services that only government can provide on a significant scale—such as education, health care, and infrastructure—there is little chance of instigating major, sustainable change in remote and poor communities.

Need for partnerships

For ICDP design and implementation, the above factors point strongly to the need for partnerships between different types of organizations. Two types of partnership can be envisioned—between development and conservation NGOs and between NGOs and government agencies. International development agencies can play an important role in facilitating and encouraging these partnerships, particularly in encouraging government agencies to participate.

The need for such partnerships is one of the strongest conclusions to emerge from this study.

8. Measuring effectiveness

Several criteria could be used to evaluate integrated conservation-development projects (ICDPs). One approach might be to build on the indexes used to monitor and evaluate rural development projects, such as target populations' incomes and wealth, literacy, productivity, and nutrition and health. Another approach would be to assess the effectiveness of projects in eliciting the participation of local people in project activities and in promoting institutions to facilitate local decisionmaking.

But these approaches are based on measures of the *means* and not the *end product;* they do not adequately measure progress against the ultimate goal. Every ICDP must eventually face the test of whether it has contributed to the conservation of biological diversity by improving the prospects for survival of the targeted protected area. Indexes of ICDP effectiveness must therefore include key ecological features, as well as the more familiar social and economic development variables.

The effectiveness of an ICDP is likely to be constrained by the scaling of the project in relation to both the protected area and the surrounding population. The protected areas targeted by the case studies vary in size from a few square kilometers to several thousand square kilometers. Other things being equal, protecting larger reserves may be expected to be more difficult than protecting smaller reserves. But, regardless of a protected area's size, ICDPs that target only a small proportion of the local population are unlikely to have a significant conservation impact.

Evaluating the effectiveness of a project requires comparing initial goals with subsequent progress toward them, as reported by project monitoring systems. These steps should be followed:

• Assess the effects of ICDP activities on people outside protected area boundaries.
• Assess the status of the plants and animals inside the protected area, and changes in their status since the ICDP began.

• Attempt to identify any causal links between changes in conditions inside protected areas and project initiatives outside—in particular the extent to which changes inside are attributable to project activities as opposed to exogenous events and processes.

Changes outside protected areas

The Boscosa (Costa Rica) and Khao Yai (Thailand) projects surveyed people living in the villages where the project was to be implemented to establish baseline data against which to measure subsequent project effects. None of the other case study projects has systematically monitored the effects of its development activities on local people. Few conducted baseline surveys, and little relevant data have been produced to quantify project benefits to individuals or communities. The few external evaluations have all been based on qualitative analysis. As a result, it has not been feasible to produce an economic or financial evaluation of any project. The analyses of local social and economic changes since the projects began (summarized in chapters 5 and 6) have thus been based mainly on informal sources and interviews, supplemented by project reports.

Changes inside protected areas

Protected area management agencies in developing countries generally lack adequate resources for systematic monitoring, particularly in large protected areas. Exceptions include occasional studies associated with the preparation of park management plans, periodic inventories of plants and animals by visiting researchers, and aerial counts of large mammals in African savanna parks.

Only three case study protected areas included a component designed to compensate for this absence of basic ecological data. All three are African savanna ecosystems dominated by large mammals

(Amboseli, Kenya; Lupande/ADMADE, Zambia; and Nazinga, Burkina Faso). In the remaining cases, it was difficult to assess what changes had taken place in wildlife and wildlands, which of these changes resulted from human activities, or whether the trends have been positive or negative.

In the case of large-scale forest conversion or agricultural encroachment, such as at Andohahela (Madagascar) and Gunung Leuser (Indonesia), or in the case of very small reserves, such as Beza Mahafaly (Madagascar) and Bururi (Burundi), adverse trends were usually obvious, even if unquantified. In other cases, the estimates of destructive and illegal activities inside park boundaries range from nonexistent through anecdotal to informed guesswork. Despite the relative lack of scientific data, informal project reports combined with the results of interviews with villagers, project personnel, park officials and their field staff, and visiting researchers have persuasively suggested that destructive and illegal activities inside protected area boundaries have diminished at several sites since the ICDPs began. These improvements appear to be associated with the following factors:

- *More effective enforcement.* This has been achieved by hiring appropriately equipped and supervised park guards, and resettling people from within the protected area boundaries—changes effected by the park authorities and by the implementers of the ICDP (Air-Tenere, Niger; Amboseli, Kenya; Bururi, Burundi; Chitwan, Nepal; Dumoga-Bone, Indonesia; Lupande/ ADMADE, Zambia; Nazinga, Burkina Faso; and Volcanoes, Rwanda). In several of these cases there is considerable local resentment and hostility toward the parks.
- *Mitigation of the adverse effects of tourism.* The Annapurna (Nepal) project has substantially reduced deforestation rates within the multiple-use conservation area by persuading the owners of small lodges to burn kerosene instead of wood as their principal energy source. At Air-Tenere (Niger), tourists have been required to travel with guides to minimize their impact.
- *Results of specific agreements.* Local communities and project representatives have agreed that investments in local development would follow from the establishment of a protected area. Examples have included repair of a road, construction of a school, and the promise of an irrigation project, all at Beza Mahafaly (Madagascar), and land titling at Talamanca (Costa Rica).

- *Direct linkage of conservation goals to development benefits.* Although many projects attempted to provide local communities with benefits, few projects established a direct linkage between the conservation aim and the benefits received by local communities. The Lupande/ADMADE (Zambia) program is an exception. More local employment, increased meat for local consumption, and revenue sharing for development are directly tied to wildlife protection.

At the remaining sites there was little evidence of change in what appear to be extremely high levels of destructive and illegal activities.

Linking inside with outside

With the limited quantity of information available from project monitoring and evaluation, it is extremely difficult for external reviewers to establish ex-post causal relationships between events inside and outside protected area boundaries. Of greater concern is that few of the case study projects have effectively made that connection. While chapter 5 describes how several of the projects have generated social and economic benefits for local people, it is questionable whether many of these benefits led to improved park security.

The Annapurna (Nepal), Beza Mahafaly (Madagascar), and Lupande/ADMADE (Zambia) projects provided the only unambiguous examples of effective and positive linkages between conservation inside and development activities outside park boundaries. Some of the case studies where such linkages were missing or ambiguous are described in box 8.1.

It might be argued that ICDPs promoting general social and economic development in local communities would not expect to observe specific links between individual program components and improved people-park interaction. And in some cases, once-hostile relations between park personnel and local communities have improved substantially because of the mediation of project personnel. Nonetheless, the development components of ICDPs have been influential in reducing threats to protected areas only in a few cases. During start-up, project staff may need to spend considerable time establishing a positive relationship with local people, particularly in areas with a history of people-park tension. In such cases, linkages may not readily be apparent even though vital preparatory work is going on to build trust and goodwill

---

Box 8.1 Ambiguous or missing linkages between the development components of projects and their conservation objectives

Amboseli, Kenya. The reserve is apparently healthy, particularly in comparison with other East African parks, despite the project's failure to achieve its objectives in fifteen years.

Khao Yai, Thailand. Low-interest loans to members of village environmental protection societies on the condition that park regulations be respected have considerably reduced individual debt burdens. It is not at all clear, however, that this has resulted in reduced poaching or logging in the adjacent national park.

Luangwa Integrated Rural Development Project (LIRDP), Zambia. Although LIRDP is similar to ADMADE, it is a broadly based integrated rural development project with fishery, agriculture, road construction, and community service components. Funding for these activities depends mainly on wildlife use and trophy fees. The ADMADE program has managed to clearly link the local benefits to wildlife, but the LIRDP project disperses funds to all of the project activities. It is thus unclear whether the link between wildlife and development can be made clear in the eyes of local people.

Monarch, Mexico. Local people receive gate receipts from tourists visiting the butterflies. Yet this has not prevented the local residents from logging in the reserve. In this case, the direct benefits from a conservation area have been insufficient to become an incentive to reduce pressure on the protected area.

Sian Ka'an, Mexico. Lobster fishermen, who claimed that land inside the park was rightfully theirs when they wanted to earn additional income from farming, posed a potentially significant threat to the reserve. Amigos de Sian Ka'an, the nongovernmental organization running the project, developed an intensive agricultural farm to demonstrate that high levels of production could be achieved on small parcels, thus partly negating the fishermen's claims. The fishermen lost their interest in farming, and the demonstration farm continues even though it is too far from local communities to be useful for training them.

Note: Other examples are described in chapter 5 and the appendix.

---

locally and thereby provide a basis for future linkages.

The argument that conservation will automatically be strengthened by improving the living standards or increasing the incomes of people outside park boundaries is appealing—and the principal justification for ICDPs. However, the case study analyses demonstrate that this argument is simplistic and that projects need to establish explicit linkages between their development components and their conservation objectives.

Scale of projects

Assessing the scale of an ICDP must begin with the physical size of the protected area targeted by the project. The variations in size of the case study protected areas was considerable, from the 65,000 square kilometer Air-Tenere National Nature Reserve in Niger to the 6 square kilometer Beza Mahafaly Special Reserve in Madagascar and the 5 square kilometer Monarch Butterfly Overwintering Reserve in Mexico (table 2.1).

Three project design features can be used to show the scale of an ICDP:

• *Geographic reach* is the area enclosed by the physical boundaries within which project activities take place. Reach need not be synonymous with the physical size of the protected area. Reach will include lands outside the protected area boundary and, in the case of multiple-use areas, may also include lands inside the overall area boundaries. Reach depends on the location and distribution of the intended beneficiaries and the ease of access to them.

• *Diversity* refers to the range of activities carried out by the project. Increasing the diversity may allow a wider range of threats to be addressed and increase the possibilities of finding new solutions. But greater diversity also may promote more change than local people are willing to make and add complexity to management—making failure more likely.

• *Intensity* refers to the level of effort of project activities—over a given area or directed toward a specific population. A project must generally decide how thinly to allocate its finite resources. For example, a project with a full-time, on-site project manager in each target village is more "intensive" than a project where one worker covers several villages. This is difficult, and perhaps impossible, to measure.

Using this approach, the total scale of a project can be expressed in terms of three variables: reach, diversity, and intensity. In practice, the total scale will be subject to a number of limiting constraints. The first is funding, not just the total funds obtainable but their pattern of availability over time and the extent to which lenders or donors are prepared to commit their funds. The second constraint is management capacity, the ability of implementing organizations—whether government agencies or nongovernmental organizations—to effectively manage a project. Third is the availability of adequately trained and experienced personnel to staff a project. The fourth constraint is a project's political acceptability—locally and nationally.

A project may need to make trade-offs among reach, diversity, and intensity. For example, a project with an inadequate reach can have little hope of having a significant effect on a protected area, because only a small proportion of the target population has even the possibility of being affected by the project. But, with an extended reach, a diverse project becomes difficult to manage. A range of varied activities carried out over a large area affecting many different communities will be difficult to coordinate. Rural development projects along these lines have tended to suffer organizational failures. Finally, with limited funds and limited staff resources, reach and intensity can be trade-offs. For example, at Khao Yai, Thailand, one of the project nongovernmental organizations has emphasized intensity (working intensively in a few villages), while the other, with pressure from donors, has emphasized reach (visiting and working in many more villages). As an illustrative example, box 8.2 tentatively applies this approach to an assessment of the scale of some of the case study projects.

How far should a project's geographic reach be, or how far should activities extend beyond the protected area boundaries? There is no single answer to this question. The appropriate scale for a project depends on site-specific aspects of the socioeconomic context and on the level and intensity of threats to the protected area. Some of the variables discussed in this section (especially intensity and diversity) cannot be measured precisely. They may, nonetheless, be useful for evaluating the adequacy of ICDPs.

Constraints inhibiting scale increases are financial, human (for project planning, management, and staffing), institutional (absorptive capacities of the implementing organizations), technological (better methods for resource use), and distributional (directing benefits to local people). The scale of most of the case study projects has been too small in relation to the protected areas or to the surrounding populations to have had a significant effect. Some of the projects are targeting small parks, and others are pilot initiatives next to larger parks. But apart from small-scale replications within ICDPs, few of the organizations that initiated or implemented these pilots have shown the inclination or capacity to promote replication.

Box 8.2 Comparing the scale of case study projects

Using the method described in the text, three ICDPs might be compared as follows:

	Reach	*Intensity*	*Diversity*
Dumoga-Bone, Indonesia	high	high	low
East Usambara, Tanzania	moderate	moderate	high
Khao Yai, Thailand			
Population and Development			
Association, Sup Tai	low	high	high
Wildlife Fund Thailand (TEAM)	high	low	high

Dumoga-Bone, Indonesia. The eastern half of this 3,000 square kilometer park drains into the Dumoga valley. The park was established to protect the upper watershed of two large irrigation projects. As a result, 12,000 farmers have been able to grow paddy rice. The Dumoga-Bone irrigation projects reach throughout a large river valley (*reach* = high), affect almost all of the land and people in the valley (*intensity* = high), and have a single objective, irrigated rice cultivation (*diversity* = low).

East Usambara, Tanzania. About 40,000 people in twenty-five to thirty villages live among sixteen small forest reserves totaling 160 square kilometers. The forests have been degraded by logging and shifting cultivation. The project is working in fifteen of the villages close to the reserves on a variety of small-scale rural development initiatives and promoting more intensive cash crop alternatives to shifting cultivation. The East Usambara project reaches almost half of the villages located among the forest reserves (*reach* = moderate), has a paid coordinator in each village (*intensity* = moderate), and has pursued a diverse range of activities (*diversity* = high). (See chapter 3.)

Khao Yai, Thailand. This 2,200 square kilometer park is surrounded by more than 100 villages. The original project started in one village on the northern boundary, Sup Tai, and was a joint effort of two nongovernmental organizations—the Population and Development Association and Wildlife Fund Thailand. All subsequent activities have been based on some variation of the Sup Tai model. Wildlife Fund Thailand dropped out of Sup Tai and began the TEAM project on the park's eastern boundary. This project focused on two groups of five villages, with a headquarters and field manager in one village in each of the two groups. Mobile education activities were planned for forty more villages. The Population and Development Association continues the project at Sup Tai and has expanded into two other nearby villages, with plans for expansion into three further villages starting in 1990. The Khao Yai projects *reach* only a small proportion of the villages that threaten the national park (*reach* = low). The Sup Tai project has several full-time, on-site staff (*intensity* = high) and has attempted a wide range of activities (*diversity* = high). The TEAM project is similarly diverse but has fewer staff trying to work in more villages (*intensity* = low). (This project is more fully described in chapter 3.)

Applying the same variables to some of the other case studies:

	Reach	*Intensity*	*Diversity*
Air-Tenere, Niger	moderate	moderate	moderate
Amboseli, Kenya			
National Park	high	moderate	low
Wildlife Extension	high	low	low
Annapurna, Nepal			
Stage I	moderate	high	high
Stage II	high	moderate	high
Beza Mahafaly, Madagascar	moderate	high	moderate
Lupande/ADMADE, Zambia	moderate	high	low
Osa/Boscosa, Costa Rica	moderate	moderate	high
Sian Ka'an, Mexico	low	low	moderate
Talamanca, Costa Rica	high	moderate	high

At their current level of operations, the Amboseli Wildlife Extension (Kenya), Andohahela (Madagascar), Khao Yai (Thailand), Monarch and Amigos de Sian Ka'an (Mexico), and Talamanca (Costa Rica) projects all appear to be too small in relation to the area they are trying to protect or the surrounding population they are hoping to influence. These ICDPs should thus be considered pilot projects.

9. Conclusions and recommendations

This study of integrated conservation-development projects (ICDPS) was expected to identify local development strategies that are compatible with ecosystem conservation, local incentives that most effectively discourage threats to parks, the best ways to involve local people in protected area management, and the types of organizations that best facilitate these approaches.

These questions remain largely unanswered. Concise, clear-cut lessons for replicating existing projects did not emerge. Instead, what stands out most clearly is that the problems that individual ICDPS are attempting to address are enormous, complex, and variable. By comparison, the pioneering efforts examined in this study appear small indeed. Many projects have annual budgets of less than $100,000—some considerably less—and few have received funding totaling more than $1 million. By development project funding standards, these amounts are very small. More fundamentally, these projects are small in terms of the influence they can exert over the forces threatening protected ecosystems. This inability to change the parameters of the environment in which they are operating appears to be the projects' greatest weakness.

Many of the factors leading to the loss of biodiversity and the degradation of protected natural ecosystems originate far from park boundaries. They include public ownership of extensive areas of land, unmatched by the capacity of government agencies to manage the land; powerful financial incentives that encourage overexploitation of timber, wildlife, grazing lands, and crop lands; an absence of linkages between the needs of conservation and the factors encouraging development; and laws, policies, social changes, and economic forces over which poor people in remote rural areas have no influence.

Addressing these issues in a meaningful way would require engaging the highest levels of governments throughout the industrialized and de-

veloping worlds and mobilizing resources on a much larger scale than has been done so far. Now, even under the best of conditions, ICDPS centered on protected areas and targeting local populations can play only a modest role in mitigating the powerful forces causing environmental degradation. When, in addition, these projects are trying to develop new approaches while relying on tiny budgets, inexperienced implementing organizations (often dependent on one or two key individuals), and limited access to usable technology, and when, furthermore, the projects are constantly struggling for official recognition, their ambitions must realistically be limited.

In these circumstances the achievements of the case study projects are perhaps remarkable. Within relatively short periods of time, several projects have established components that appear promising and that have elicited a measure of support among the local population. Although measurable progress has been rare, early experiences of the case study ICDPS offer some valuable lessons for future initiatives in this area.

Are integrated conservation-development projects necessary?

Most of the analysis to this point has emphasized how challenging and complex ICDP implementation can be: how necessary it is to understand the socioeconomic context of each project; how important it is to elicit local participation; how difficult it is to promote social and economic development in remote rural communities; how limited is the capacity to participate of most government protected area management agencies; and so on. This study has reviewed the early experiences of more than twenty projects and found that progress has been very modest. One might well ask, why bother? Why promote the expansion of a concept that appears to be so difficult to put into practice? If the commitment to conserve biodiversity is sincere, then the answer is that ICDP approaches must be reinforced and expanded simply because there are few viable alternatives.

Increasing resource demands from growing rural populations and continuing large-scale conversion or degradation of natural ecosystems will exert ever-increasing pressure on parks and reserves. While traditional enforcement will continue to play a critical role—and in many cases needs desperately to be strengthened—it is inconceivable that networks of protected areas can be maintained indefinitely by what amounts, in some cases, to military force. This leads to the conclusion that *innovative, well-designed ICDPs at carefully selected sites that constructively address local people-park relationships are essential to the conservation of biodiversity and thus to sustainable development.*

This is not to say that even successful ICDPs can alone conserve biodiversity. The other initiatives and policy measures that are needed have been well described by others, notably McNeely and colleagues (1990).

Lessons for the future

This chapter, drawing on earlier discussions and findings, sets out the lessons from this study for future design and implementation of ICDPs. These lessons have been grouped into seven areas: (1) projects as part of a larger framework, (2) scale of projects, (3) organizations participating in projects, (4) project site selection, (5) local participation in projects, (6) financial resources of projects, and (7) project design and implementation.

The lessons presented below are in descending priority. This is to emphasize that lessons in the final area—on-the-ground project design and implementation—although critical to project effectiveness, are likely to prove considerably easier to apply than those emerging from the other five areas. In fact, failure to effectively address the lessons in the other areas is likely to leave barriers that will frustrate even the best design and implementation efforts.

Projects as part of a larger framework

It has become clear from the case studies that ICDPs have been implemented on too narrow a front. Conserving biodiversity in protected areas cannot be regarded solely as an issue of protected land management, even if that management has been expanded and reoriented as part of an ICDP to include park neighbors.

Threats to parks and their neighbors often originate far from park boundaries. Local people, the intended beneficiaries of ICDPs, are commonly the most visible agents of park degradation; however, their actions are often attributable to laws, policies, patterns of resource access, social changes, and economic forces—factors that ICDPs and their sponsors can have little hope of influencing. Furthermore, many of the case study ICDPs have proved vulnerable to external events that have caused project operations to be suspended or have led directly to protected area degradation on a large scale. These have included commodity price collapses in several countries (leading to very high local unemployment and hardship), guerilla warfare in Peru, kerosene shortages in Nepal, land price escalation in Thailand, a debt-related budget crisis in Kenya, and the ivory ban that threatened to reduce hunting revenues in Zambia.

It is not likely—or even desirable—that ICDP managers will ever have control over, or even be able to influence, all of the parameters of the environment in which they operate. However, field experience has highlighted certain aspects of this external environment that appear fundamental to project effectiveness. These can be used to derive a series of project preconditions. Although these preconditions are not universally applicable, this study suggests the need for caution before proceeding with an ICDP in the absence of any of them. These preconditions include:

- *Serious political commitments to the project.* Explicit commitments to support, or at least cooperate with, the ICDP must be obtained in advance from local authorities, from influential local leaders, and from high levels within appropriate agencies of the national government—including all agencies with relevant interests and authority.
- *Legislation conducive to the achievement of ICDP objectives.* Jurisdiction over lands outside park boundaries is often unclear and can provide a significant barrier to ICDP implementation. Legislative reform will often be needed to give ICDPs, park management agencies, or both, the authority to act outside existing park boundaries; to clarify overlapping authorities over lands adjacent to parks among local governments and national government agencies; to establish multiple-use areas that include conservation (protected) and development (human-use) zones; to establish buffer zones outside the boundaries of existing traditional parks; to delegate government authority over a traditional park or a multiple-use area to a separate ICDP man-

agement organization; or to provide for a share of park entry and concession fees to go to the parks system, or be passed through the ICDP to local communities.

- *Realistic institutional arrangements for project management.* Where appropriate, new management structures should be empowered to represent different national and local interests involved in the ICDP, including collaboration with the protected area management agencies, if local park management is to remain administratively separate from the project. These arrangements could include explicit authorization for ICDPs implemented by appropriately qualified nongovernmental organizations and, possibly, the delegation of limited park-management authority to these organizations.

- *Compatibility with regional development.* Project development components should ideally be coordinated with regional development initiatives. At the very least there should be effective communication between regional development planners and the ICDPs. Particular care will need to be taken to avoid the establishment of an "attraction zone" that draws new migrants close to a heavily subsidized, rapidly developing area close to a park, and to avoid environmentally damaging regional development projects that threaten to undermine the ICDP and the protected area (such as uncontrolled development).

- *Systematic attention to land ownership and other resource access rights of the projects' intended beneficiaries.* Lack of secure tenure has prevented many ICDPs from persuading settlers or recent migrants to adopt a long-term perspective toward land management, including more intensive cultivation outside park boundaries. Priority should thus be given to clarifying or establishing secure land tenure and resource access for individuals and communities living adjacent to park boundaries.

- *Commitment to institutional reorientation.* Government agencies responsible for traditional-park management face considerable constraints in implementing ICDPs or supporting ICDPs implemented by other organizations, even with funding and technical assistance from international organizations. Many of these agencies require strengthening and reorientation toward a more people-centered approach.

Scale of projects

Small-scale ICDPs are appropriate to relatively small parks or those under little threat from surrounding populations. But to have a significant effect on larger protected areas in developing countries, more substantial initiatives will be needed. Most ICDPs are operating on a scale considerably smaller than that of the immediate problems they are trying to address, and even the larger ICDPs are small by development project standards (chapter 8).

Small ICDPs can be considered to have made a significant contribution to biodiversity conservation only if their experiences provide the basis for replication on a larger scale, either by expanding to include more communities or more development activities around their targeted protected areas, or by launching new and more substantial projects at additional sites. Thus far, such replication has been rare (and governments appear to have tolerated some of the ICDPs implemented by nongovernmental organizations only because the projects have remained so small). This is not the fault of the implementing organizations. Many of these groups and agencies have been extended to their limits by the original project and lack the resources to scale up. Quite appropriately, many of these organizations view experimenting with this new approach as their major contribution, a role to which they are aptly suited; they regard expansion and replication as the task of others.

The scale of ICDPs must be expanded cautiously. Many rural development efforts have collapsed as a result of attempting to expand too quickly, placing impossible demands on local leadership and institutions, and becoming far removed from their intended beneficiaries. The management structures of large projects can become so complex that decisionmaking becomes rigid. Large projects in a relatively small and underfinanced sector such as biodiversity conservation can also attract a disproportionately large share of available financial, human, and institutional resources—to the detriment of protected areas elsewhere in the country.

These dangers are now relatively well-known, even though some development projects continue to disregard them. Unless these risks are overcome and the scale of ICDP operations is substantially increased, prospects for biodiversity conservation will continue to deteriorate.

Participating organizations

ICDP implementation has been assisted by government agencies, conservation and development nongovernmental organizations, and development agencies. Each type of organization has important contributions to make. However, the experiences of the case study projects demonstrate that, working independently, none of these organizations can effectively plan and implement ICDPs (chapter 7). One of the clearest lessons from this study is that implementation of the next generation of ICDP initiatives linking ecosystem protection with local economic development needs to involve significantly larger collaboration among governments, conservation groups, development nongovernmental organizations, development organizations, and aid agencies.

Partnerships provide a basis for effectively addressing the challenge that distinguishes ICDPs from all other conservation or development projects: the need to link socioeconomic development with biodiversity conservation. Two types of partnership will be particularly important in project design and implementation: partnerships between development and conservation nongovernmental organizations, and partnerships between these nongovernmental organizations and government agencies.

The need to fit ICDPs into a larger development framework has already been emphasized. Nongovernmental organizations and government agencies charged with protected area management can play only a limited role in this process. High-level commitment and involvement from governments will also be necessary. International development agencies such as the World Bank can facilitate—and possibly finance—these partnerships, particularly by encouraging the appropriate individuals and organizations to participate.

In many cases, the organizations available to play key roles in ICDPs have institutional weaknesses. For example, the government agencies responsible for protected area management tend to be politically weak and to lack resources, equipment, and adequately trained personnel—making it extremely difficult for them to carry out basic management, let alone participate effectively in ICDPs. In such cases, organizational strengthening, and possibly reorientation, will be an important priority—one that donors have tended to avoid in favor of discrete projects.

Site selection

Should an ICDP be established in association with every protected area? Absolutely not. The ICDP approach is clearly not only experimental but complex, time-consuming, and expensive, requiring a complex mix of inputs. This suggests that the next generation of full-scale ICDPs should give highest priority to (although not necessarily be limited to)

protected areas in countries that have already made significant progress in establishing protected area networks and the institutions to manage them, that have outstanding ecological significance, and that have local site conditions that threaten the viability of the protected ecosystems but appear favorable to successful project implementation.

What local site conditions can be considered favorable for ICDP implementation? In general, favorable conditions would include

- Relatively low or, at least, stable population densities (if population densities are judged too high or are in biologically sensitive areas, consideration may need to be given to resettlement)
- Widespread use of traditional or appropriate technologies for resource extraction
- Protected areas where effective management is already in place
- Local leaders and responsible central government agencies willing to cooperate
- Participation of capable organizations, probably in partnerships as described above.

Sites not meeting these criteria may require different approaches.

Local participation

Eliciting authentic participation in projects is difficult and time-consuming in developed countries and even more so in developing nations. But evidence from ICDPs has confirmed one of the principal lessons from rural development projects: that the sustainability of project benefits depends strongly on the effective participation of local people. This means more than participation as project beneficiaries or as paid employees. It means participation in decisionmaking, in problem identification, in project design and implementation, and in project monitoring and evaluation. This approach views local development as a process rather than a product, with project personnel performing a facilitating role. Establishment of a process of local participation has proved to be a more effective method of sustaining project benefits (and therefore more cost-effective on a long-term basis) than approaches that attempt to deliver economic benefits without involving local people or building community commitment to the outcome of the project.

Some projects have shown signs of promise in winning the trust and confidence of local people, eliciting the participation of community members in project-initiated activities, and starting institutions for local resource-management decisionmaking. Several promising local organizations have been formed to manage resources. However, although some of these institutions and the networks of field workers established by the projects have attracted local backing, very few are independent of the projects. Without operational independence, achieving ICDP goals and sustaining benefits once a project has finished will be difficult (chapter 6).

Financial recources

Much more money is needed, and over a considerably longer period of time. While more money resources will not automatically overcome many of the constraints identified in this study, ICDPs will not be able to expand to the scale needed to make a significant impact without large, long-term donor commitments.

As development practitioners have learned, the rapid scaling up of complex projects is rarely successful because it overwhelms the absorptive capacities of the implementing organizations and the intended beneficiaries. This study has also observed that long periods are needed to elicit local participation in projects, an ICDP prerequisite, particularly if new local institutions are to be established.

These factors all suggest that annual project funding needs will build up slowly over several years from fairly low levels, in contrast to conventional donor financing preferences for projects that use loan and grant funds fairly rapidly. Large one-time financial inputs or short-term grants for ICDPs should thus be avoided. Furthermore, it is usually unrealistic to expect that these projects will become financially self-sufficient or that their recurrent costs will be financed by governments after a few years.

Project design and implementation

Several ICDPs have suffered from severe design and implementation flaws. Some of these problems are attributable to the new and complex challenges of ICDPs; others result from a failure to consider the well-documented lessons from decades of rural development programs of both development agencies and development-oriented nongovernmental organizations (chapter 4). The most serious problems noted among the case study projects were the following:

- Most projects were designed without adequate understanding of the socioeconomic context. Although useful knowledge was gained by capable field staff during project execution, it did not compensate for a lack of baseline data collection. "Quick-and-dirty" data collection and analysis methods, such as rapid rural appraisal, were rarely used (chapter 2).

- There was a general failure to specify exactly how ICDP development activities were expected to lead to enhanced protected area management. The ICDP approach has to be judged by whether development has improved the security of protected areas and whether local people have come to accept the existence of the protected area. In virtually all projects, the critical linkage between development and conservation has been missing or unclear (chapter 4).

- Few projects have identified viable alternatives to the extensive resource-use practices that threaten many protected areas. Rural development in general lacks site-specific technical options, particularly in drier areas; nonetheless, the case study projects have made few attempts to use indigenous knowledge and technologies, and few of the projects have conducted systematic experiments to identify new options (chapter 5).

- Very few of the projects appeared likely to generate enough economic or financial benefits to become self-sufficient. Deriving significant economic benefits from areas that lack tourism potential has proved extremely difficult. Areas where nature tourism can finance conservation or provide benefits to local people remain limited. Most biologically important areas do not have the potential for enough tourism to support conservation. And at sites where tourism revenues are high, the benefits tend to be captured by the private sector in major cities or by central treasury funds (chapter 5).

- The social and economic benefits flowing to local people as a result of ICDP development activities are difficult to identify and are unevenly—sometimes narrowly—distributed. There is little evidence that those benefiting represent threats to the parks, and there are few examples of those threatening the parks—usually the poorest and the landless—receiving enough benefits to reduce their potential threat (chapter 5).

- When projects have provided or subsidized community services, such as schools and health clinics, links between the service and protected area management objectives have not always been clear. Projects that required a local contribution of cash or labor to community services had more positive results than those that donated goods or services (chapter 5).

• Most of the ICDP field staff, whether expatriates or nationals, have been experienced, well-trained, energetic, and knowledgeable. Positive relationships have been developed with local people, many of whom were distrustful, if not outright hostile, when the projects began. Project field workers frequently have personified the projects locally—and their leadership and counsel were obviously valued in many of the targeted communities. Careful attention will have to be paid to how these projects will continue under local control after these charismatic leaders leave (chapter 6).

• Projects have given little attention to monitoring and evaluation. Very few projects monitor the effects of their development activities and most could provide no information on changes in a targeted protected area (chapter 8).

• There were few, if any, working examples of a buffer zone. Although conceptually attractive and potentially useful, the buffer zone remains ill-defined in practice, particularly without specific enabling legislation (chapter 2).

• Many nongovernmental organizations implementing the smaller projects on the boundaries of existing protected areas have been unable to establish constructive relationships with the protected area managers. This contributed to a separation between development and conservation aspects of the projects (chapter 7).

• The design of several projects apparently was based on unjustified assumptions. In particular, it is clear that project implementers should not assume that communities can be induced to change their use of park lands rapidly; that superior technological options are available to intensify agriculture or that people will automatically adopt them if the options are there; that local institutions for resource management can easily be established; that change on a significant scale can be brought about without government involvement; or that providing local jobs or financing community services is equivalent to local participation (chapter 4).

A final word

For the initiatives collectively described here as integrated conservation-development projects to play a significant role in conserving biological diversity, decisive actions need to be taken, jointly and separately, by implementing organizations, national governments, and lenders and donors—including international development agencies. Without deliberate, concerted actions by these groups—including the organizations represented by the authors—the outlook for biodiversity in developing countries will be bleak. The long gestation periods that ICDPs need clearly mandate that these actions be taken sooner rather than later.

The challenge is not just to implement more effective ICDPs. That should be feasible, although it will require more financial support and creative modifications of existing approaches, with a more thorough understanding of rural development. The greater challenge will be to engage the individuals and organizations with the commitment and capacity to establish social, economic, legal, and institutional environments that facilitate—instead of frustrate—achievement of ICDP biodiversity conservation goals.

Education.

Appendix
Case study summaries

Africa

Burkina Faso, Nazinga Game Ranch

Protected area. The 1,000 square kilometer Nazinga Game Ranch.

Project. The Nazinga Game Ranch.

Implementing organization. The African Wildlife Husbandry Development Association, a nongovernmental organization formed by expatriates to establish and manage the ranch, in partnership with the government.

Responsible government agency. Ministry of Environment and Tourism.

Funding. From 1979-89, the project received a total of $3.1 million in grants from the Canadian International Development Agency and contributions of land and salary support from the government of Burkina Faso.

Project area and scope. The project has focused on habitat and antipoaching measures to restore wildlife populations for safari hunting and the game meat production inside the ranch boundaries.

Region. The idea for the ranch originated during the 1972-74 Sahel drought, although major funding did not become available until 1979.

Project activities. The original project goals were to research, design, and develop rational use of wildlife resources in the region, to increase the resources, and to benefit the local people. Antipoaching measures and the establishment of water points were an early priority. Extensive housing facilities and 600 kilometers of roads were constructed by 1984, employing substantial numbers of local people. The project did not begin harvesting for meat production until 1989.

Tourism and safari operations, although successful revenue earners for the ranch, have not yet brought much benefit to local populations. In spite of the ranch's focus on game production, the single greatest benefit realized by local populations has

been a substantial increase in fishing opportunities. The creation of numerous permanent water points about the ranch has greatly increased the number and species of fish. The ranch has implemented a fisheries management program to regulate access to fishing rights.

In late 1989 the Ministry of Environment and Tourism assumed full control of the ranch and the participation of the African Wildlife Husbandry Development Association was ended.

Evaluation. The permanent water points and routine antipoaching patrols were key factors in the reported threefold increase in wildlife populations between 1981 and 1984. The project has been very successful in improving wildlife habitat and increasing wildlife populations. This success was the result of a sound research program and a two-pronged approach to protection: antipoaching activities and environmental improvement (dam construction, and pasture and fire management). In other words, the project has succeeded in devising and implementing technical solutions to specific problems. Benefits to local people have, however, been limited to direct employment.

Burundi, Bururi Forest Reserve

Protected area. The Bururi Forest Reserve comprises about 20 square kilometers. About 16 square kilometers of the reserve remain in natural forest; the remainder is deforested and is now in pine plantations.

Project. Bururi Forest project.

Implementing organization. The government of Burundi, with voluntary assistance provided by the U.S. Peace Corps.

Responsible government agency. National Institute of Nature Conservation of Burundi (the park service).

Funding. The Bururi Forest project was funded by a five-year grant of $1.2 million from USAID. The grant ended in 1987.

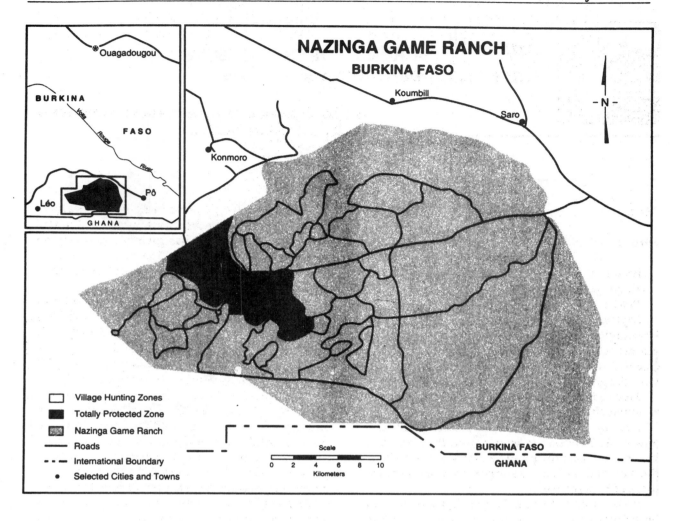

NAZINGA GAME RANCH
BURKINA FASO

- ☐ Village Hunting Zones
- ■ Totally Protected Zone
- ▨ Nazinga Game Ranch
- — Roads
- ‐‐‐ International Boundary
- • Selected Cities and Towns

Scale
0 2 4 6 8 10
Kilometers

Project area and scope. Approximately 100 square kilometers; population 4,000-5,000.

Region. The Bururi Forest project focuses on a small patch of highland forest in central Burundi that was under threat from fuelwood gathering, grazing, and agricultural encroachment. The forest had been preserved as a royal hunting area before becoming a forest reserve.

Land use around the Bururi forest is mainly subsistence agriculture. About 4,000 people live within 2 kilometers of the reserve. The forest is transected by several footpaths that are important links between outlying areas and the village of Bururi.

Project activities. The Bururi Forest project was the first donor-supported project of the Burundian National Institute of Nature Conservation. The project objective was to improve management of the Bururi forest reserve and provide alternative sources of wood products to the local community. Project activities included enforcement, education,

forestry, and agroforestry extension. The project upgraded the reserve forest guard contingent from one to eight and marked the reserve boundary. Project extension agents incorporated conservation messages in their extension discussions with local farmers, and presentations and demonstration plots were established in local primary and secondary schools. The project initially attempted to establish plantations of exotic tree species next to the reserve. Following an evaluation that pointed out the problems with such an approach, plantation forestry was de-emphasized and an agroforestry extension program developed instead.

Evaluation. The Bururi Forest project has made a major contribution to the conservation of this small reserve. Project records document a dramatic decline in reserve violations following the establishment of the agroforestry program. Several families living inside the reserve have been relocated. Project staff regard environmental education as the greatest project success. However, USAID fund-

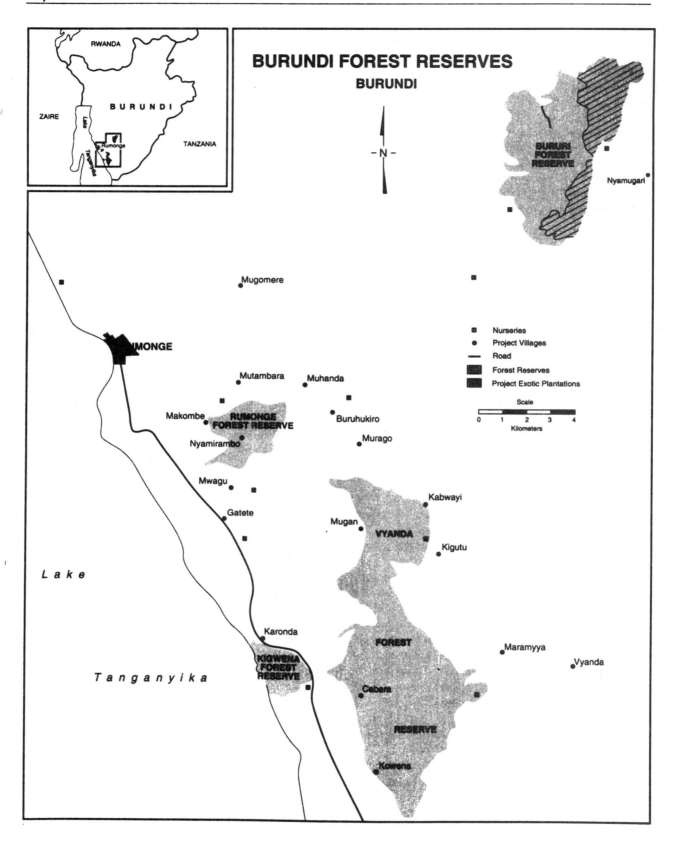

BURUNDI FOREST RESERVES
BURUNDI

- N -

BURURI FOREST RESERVE

Nyamugari

Mugomere

RUMONGE

Mutambara   Muhanda

Makombe   Buruhukiro
RUMONGE FOREST RESERVE

Nyamirambo

Murago

Mwagu

Gatete

Kabwayi

Mugan   VYANDA

Kigutu

Lake

Karonda

Maramyya

Tanganyika   KIGWENA FOREST RESERVE   FOREST

Vyanda

Cabera

RESERVE

Kawena

▣	Nurseries
●	Project Villages
—	Road
▨	Forest Reserves
▨	Project Exotic Plantations

Scale

0   1   2   3   4
Kilometers

RWANDA

ZAIRE   B U R U N D I

Lake Tanganyika   Rumonge   TANZANIA

ing was phased out in 1987 and the project has since faltered for lack of funds. Although agroforestry activities have been turned over to local cooperatives, the project lacks funds for even basic nursery supplies such as plastic bags for seedling distribution. The long-term implications of these recurrent cost problems for project sustainability are unclear.

Burundi, Rumonge, Vyanda, and Kigwena Reserves

Protected area. Rumonge Forest Reserve comprises 10 square kilometers; Vyanda Forest Reserve, 40 square kilometers; and Kigwena Forest Reserve, 8 square kilometers.

Project. Rumonge Agroforestry project.

Implementing organization. The government of Burundi, in association with Catholic Relief Services.

Responsible government agency. National Institute of Nature Conservation of Burundi.

Funding. Catholic Relief Services has provided project funding through several grants spanning five years and amounting to approximately $500,000.

Project area and scope. The project works in eight villages surrounding three protected areas. Total project area is over 100 square kilometers, with a population of more than 3,000 people.

Region. The local economy is fairly diverse, with agriculture supplemented by fishing and trading opportunities on nearby Lake Tanganyika. The project is trying to replicate the approach developed at Bururi. The project is attempting to strengthen protection of the three reserves and to provide alternative sources of wood products, employment, and income to local communities.

Project activities. As at Bururi, the major emphasis is on reserve management and agroforestry. Six reserve guards have been hired—the first full-time guards assigned to any of the reserves. With the assistance of local government the project has relocated thirty families living illegally in the reserves. An agroforestry extension program has distributed tree seedlings through a network of extension agents and model farmers; this network also serves as a channel for environmental education. To help promote tourism, the project has built trails for visitors, has trained guides, and has developed tourism plans for the area.

Evaluation. The project was up and running relatively quickly because of its reliance on the agroforestry and enforcement techniques used at Bururi. But the Rumonge reserves, although small

in absolute terms, cover a larger area than the Bururi reserve, and forest degradation is more severe. To reduce the problems with recurrent costs encountered at Bururi, efforts are being made to develop revenue-generating activities within the project. Whether these actions will ensure the sustainability of this larger and more ambitious project will become clear only after external donor support ends in 1991. Significant tourism is likely to depend on successful habituation of the reserves' chimpanzees to the presence of visitors.

Kenya, Amboseli National Park

Protected area. Amboseli National Park, a 488 square kilometer savanna park important for its large mammals and permanent water.

Project. Amboseli Park Agreement.

Implementing organization. The government of Kenya, with part-time technical assistance from the New York Zoological Society.

Responsible government agency. Wildlife Conservation and Management Department.

Funding. The project was funded primarily through a $37 million World Bank concessional loan, which benefited Amboseli as part of a larger effort to foster wildlife and tourism in Kenya.

Project area and scope. The project addressed communities within several group ranches around Amboseli National Park, primarily those within 10 kilometers of the park.

Region. The Amboseli basin is an area of perennial springs at the foot of Mount Kilimanjaro. Wildlife are abundant, concentrating around springs in the dry season and dispersing to the outlying basin during the rains. The people of Amboseli are Masai pastoralists who have occupied the area for centuries. The Masai have traditionally relied on the springs of Amboseli to water their stock. The Masai hold group tenure to the land surrounding Amboseli and maintain open range, which is critical to wildlife dispersal. Amboseli National Park incorporates the largest system of springs in the basin, an area of critical importance to both livestock and wildlife in the dry season.

Project activities. Previous conservation areas (game reserve, 1906; national reserve, 1948) at Amboseli had permitted Masai use of the area. This right was removed when the national park was established, with a complex set of direct cash payments and development measures offered to the Masai in compensation. Major components of the project were water supply, direct compensation, community services, and tourism develop-

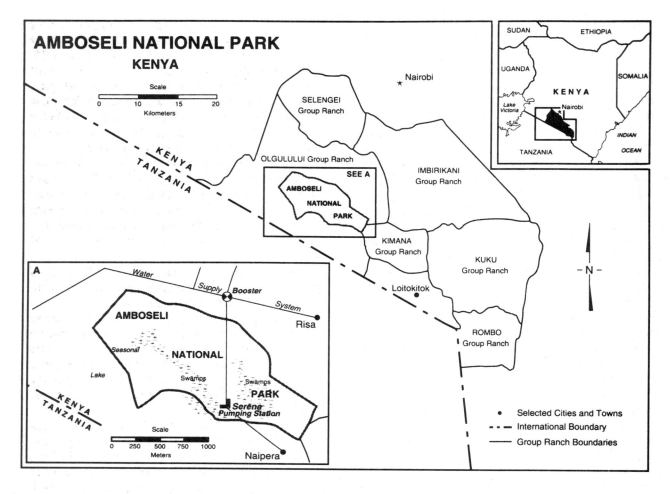

AMBOSELI NATIONAL PARK
KENYA

Selected Cities and Towns
International Boundary
Group Ranch Boundaries

ment on Masai lands. A pipeline system was constructed to provide the Masai with access to spring water without entering the park. The government agreed to pay direct compensation to the Masai, proportional to wildlife use of Masai lands. Park headquarters were relocated adjacent to Masai lands, and included a school and dispensary. The Masai were assisted in developing contracts with tourism operators for camping concessions on Masai land.

Evaluation (see Kiss 1990). Despite being one of the most cited examples of protected areas returning benefits to local communities, the goals of the Amboseli Park Agreement are still largely unrealized. The piping system has not been fully functional for more than ten years. Compensation was terminated by government financial constraints in the early 1980s. The dispensary is well-used, but the school is not. Tourism development on Masai lands has been minor. Because government commitments have not been honored, the Masai still use springs in the park to water livestock. To date, however, the Masai have received few of the benefits promised in the plan and have done little to modify their use of the park.

Kenya, Wildlife Extension project, Amboseli National Park

Protected area. Amboseli National Park lies wholly within the project area. Chyulu Hills and Tsavo West National Parks border the project area on the north and east. The project is intended to improve attitudes toward wildlife and conservation in communities bordering all three parks.

Project. Wildlife Extension project.

Implementing organization. The project is an independent activity, designed and managed by an expatriate zoologist with a social science background.

Responsible government agency. The project works closely with the regional game warden and other representatives of government, but there is no formal government involvement.

Funding. The project has received funding from several sources, with major support coming from the African Wildlife Leadership Foundation and UNESCO. Annual funding is on the order of $50,000.

Project area and scope. The project area is defined as the Loitokitok division of the Kajiado District in southern Kenya. The Loitokitok division comprises approximately 4,626 square kilometers, with a human population of approximately 30,000.

Region. The Wildlife Extension project operates in the interface between Amboseli and Tsavo West Parks in southern Kenya. The project addresses many of the same Masai communities affected by the Amboseli National Park Agreement.

Project activities. The Wildlife Extension project has focused on the needs of women, on household conservation, and on facilitating constructive relationships between wildlife officials and the community. Key project activities are educational workshops, small-scale community development projects, facilitation of government-community interface, and development of education and training materials. Community representatives attend workshops at which community needs are discussed and means of project assistance are formulated, resulting in small-scale community conservation projects. The Wildlife Extension project facilitates implementation of these projects with technical assistance and fund-raising. The project also works closely with local government officials and wildlife officers to develop an extension—as opposed to enforcement—approach to wildlife conservation. The project has produced educational materials and assisted government and university training in wildlife extension.

Evaluation. The Wildlife Extension project's human-oriented approach has produced little tangible evidence of increased community appreciation of wildlife. This is in part because of the large size of the project area (4,626 square kilometers) in relation to project staff (one director and two assistants) and funding. Volunteers who were expected to serve as the link between the project and the community have not been easily accepted in the Masai community, which has a strong emphasis on traditional leadership. The project has established good working relations with local and central government and conservation nongovernmental organizations, but the impact thus far has been insignificant.

Madagascar, Andohahela Integral Reserve and Beza Mahafaly Special Reserve Area

Protected area. The Andohahela reserve—believed to be the richest center of biodiversity in Madagascar—was established in 1939 and ex-

panded in 1966. About 40 percent of the reserve has been deforested. The 6 square kilometer Beza Mahafaly Special Reserve was established in 1985. The reserve protects a small area of southwestern Madagascar's rapidly declining riverain and spiny bush forest. The 760 square kilometer Andohahela Integral Reserve in southeast Madagascar includes a unique transition zone from the eastern rainforests into the southern spiny desert.

Project. The Conservation in Southern Madagascar project was initiated in 1977. The project primarily focused on conservation activities at Beza Mahafaly until 1985, when it expanded to include development activities at Beza Mahafaly and conservation and development activities at Andohahela.

Implementing organizations. The School of Agronomy (University of Madagascar), Yale University, and Washington University.

Responsible government agency. Both reserves are under the jurisdiction of the Nature Conservation Service within the Directory of Waters and Forests of the Ministry of Animal Husbandry, Waters, and Forests. The School of Agronomy at the University of Madagascar has been granted responsibility for Beza Mahafaly.

Funding. The World Wildlife Fund provided $120,500 during 1977-85 and $165,000 during 1985-89. USAID provided $170,000 for 1987-89, $70,000 for road construction (from public law 480 funds), and has committed $140,000 for a canal project.

Project area and scope. Villages in the immediate proximity of the reserves.

Region. In 1977, three collaborating universities sought a site in southwestern Madagascar for conservation, training, and research. People in the Beza Mahafaly area expressed an interest in protecting an area of forest that they believed to be sacred. There are eight villages within 20 kilometers of the reserve, with a total population of less than 2,000. The local Mahafaly people have taboos against killing wildlife. Maize, manioc, sweet potato, and rice are the major crops. Preliminary tests suggested that local soils could sustain agriculture for two to three decades after forest clearance.

Project activities. At Beza Mahafaly the project aimed to provide people with an incentive to support conservation efforts by making an agreement with them specifying the obligations of villagers and the benefits that they would receive. The project then sought funding to repair an important access road, renovate a 10 kilometer irrigation canal, build and equip a school, and develop a program for small-scale agricultural activities. Although the canal is not complete, the other activities have been implemented, some after very long delays. Forest guards have been hired from local villages, and the Beza Mahafaly Reserve is adequately protected.

The Andohahela project has hired eleven forest guards from local villages and has begun a series of surveys to formulate a development and conservation program that will build upon the Beza Mahafaly experience. Ten small irrigation projects have been completed, irrigating 40 hectares of land for twenty-three families. Various small-scale agricultural activities have also been initiated.

Evaluation. The relatively small Beza Mahafaly Reserve has become an important model of com-

munity involvement in conservation in Madagascar. The decision to create the reserve was made by the entire population of the valley, in anticipation of development activities to improve their livelihoods. These benefits have taken more than a decade to be delivered, and many of the activities are focused on the single village of Analafaly. The major benefit has come from road repairs, which have improved access to the nearest market town. Completion of the canal project will probably result in a significant increase in income for about 600 families. Local people have supported the project's conservation goals while receiving fairly modest development benefits in return. Several factors appear to account for this behavior: the complete absence of government services in the

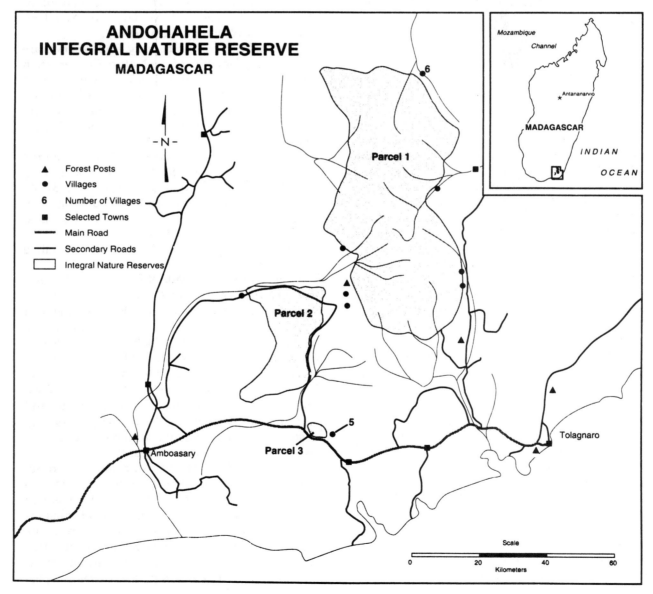

ANDOHAHELA
INTEGRAL NATURE RESERVE
MADAGASCAR

-N-

▲ Forest Posts
● Villages
6 Number of Villages
■ Selected Towns
······ Main Road
—— Secondary Roads
☐ Integral Nature Reserves

Parcel 1
Parcel 2
Parcel 3

Amboasary
Tolagnaro

Mozambique Channel
Antananarivo
MADAGASCAR
INDIAN OCEAN

Scale
0   20   40   60
Kilometers

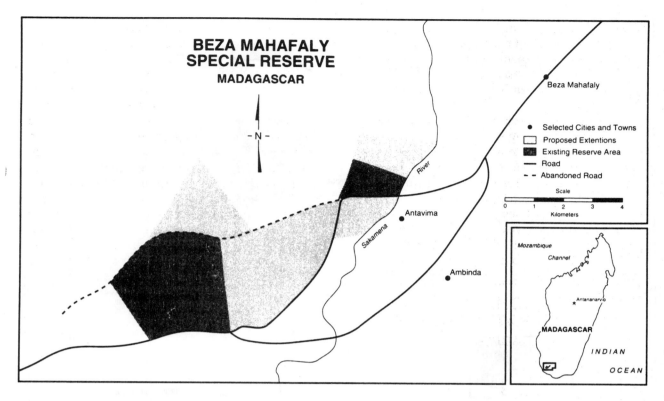

**BEZA MAHAFALY
SPECIAL RESERVE**
MADAGASCAR

- N -

Beza Mahafaly

• Selected Cities and Towns
☐ Proposed Extentions
■ Existing Reserve Area
— Road
- - Abandoned Road

Scale

0   1   2   3   4
Kilometers

River

Antavima

Sakamena

Ambinda

*Mozambique
Channel*

Antananarvio

MADAGASCAR

INDIAN

OCEAN

area, a ten-year involvement of expatriates committed to developing and maintaining a positive relationship with local communities, and an effective dialogue with government agencies. Several other factors suggest that the Beza experience would be difficult to replicate: the reserve is small; there were low population densities, stable agricultural systems, and a relative abundance of fuelwood in the vicinity of the reserve; and a relatively large number of local people were hired as forest guards.

Andohahela is more than 100 times larger than Beza Mahafaly and is surrounded by an equivalently greater population. It is too early to evaluate this project component.

Niger, Air-Tenere National Nature Reserve

Protected area. The Air-Tenere National Nature Reserve covers 65,000 square kilometers of arid lands on the southern fringes of the Sahara Desert. The Air Mountains form a plateau with peaks rising to 2,000 meters, extending into the sandy plains of the Tenere region. This exceptionally harsh environment supports several rare mammal species including the Barbary sheep, ostrich, and addax, dama, and dorcas gazelles. The reserve was established as a multiple-use area in 1988 by legislation that banned hunting but specifically allowed the resident population to remain and protected their customary resource-use rights, including fuelwood collection, harvesting of fruits and certain plants, and livestock grazing.

Project. The Air-Tenere Conservation and Management of Natural Resources project.

Implementing organizations. The World Wide Fund for Nature, the World Wildlife Fund-International, and the International Union for Conservation of Nature and Natural Resources (IUCN).

Responsible government agency. Service of Wildlife and Fisheries of the Ministry of Agriculture and Environment.

Funding. For 1982-85, $580,000. For phase I of the integrated project phase (1987-90), $2.7 million.

Project area and scope. The project began in 1982. Conservation activities have reached throughout the reserve. Recent development initiatives have focused on one of the two permanent settlements inside the reserve.

Region. This massive multiple-use area contains only 4,500 people, all of Twareg descent. The Twaregs have a benevolent attitude toward wildlife and do not represent a serious threat to the reserve's plants and animals. About half live in two villages in which the major economic activities are gardening and rearing livestock. The remainder of the population practices transhuman

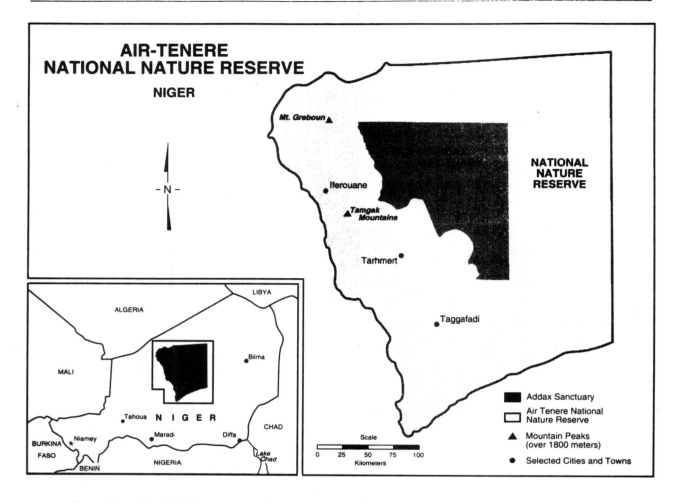

**AIR-TENERE
NATIONAL NATURE RESERVE**

NIGER

- N -

Mt. Greboun ▲

NATIONAL
NATURE
RESERVE

• Iferouane

▲ Tamgak
Mountains

Tarhmert •

• Taggafadi

■ Addax Sanctuary
□ Air Tenere National
   Nature Reserve
▲ Mountain Peaks
   (over 1800 meters)
• Selected Cities and Towns

Scale
0   25   50   75   100
Kilometers

LIBYA

ALGERIA

MALI

• Bilma

• Tahoua   N I G E R

BURKINA   * Niamey   • Maradi   • Diffa   CHAD
FASO
BENIN   NIGERIA   Lake
                  Chad

pastoralism. Though rainfall is erratic, the area's short rainy seasons maintain a subsurface water table that supports animal and vegetable life and allows for year-round irrigated gardening at the two settlements. Wildlife populations have been hurt by recurring droughts since the late 1960s, compounded by human activities. As grazing resources have dried up, trees and bushes have been damaged to provide browse for camels and goats. Soldiers have shot game animals, which have also been harrassed by foreign tourists in all-terrain vehicles.

Project activities. The project objectives include reconciling the sustained use of natural resources with conservation while promoting socioeconomic development in the region. Initial conservation activities included prevention of poaching, control of tree-cutting, surveillance of tourism, and a public awareness campaign. Research activities included wildlife censuses, resource inventories, and vegetation monitoring. Development activities in and around the permanent settlements have included efforts to rehabilitate degraded pastures,

the promotion of techniques for woodless house construction, fuel-efficient cooking stoves, and the establishment of two nurseries. Six experimental small dams for flash-flood control were well received, and several hundred more were subsequently constructed.

A volunteer network of village representatives has been established among local leaders. Their responsibilities are to be well-informed of the rules, goals, and activities in the reserve; to sensitize others to these rules and goals; and to inform the enforcement authorities of any infractions.

Evaluation. Since the reserve was established, the publicity surrounding the project, legal prohibitions against hunting, and enforcement activities of project staff have largely eliminated poaching. Wildlife populations appear to be gradually increasing. There have been no recent droughts, and so grazing regulations are thus far untested. Efforts to restore pastures have had limited success so far. Most of the villagers have benefited—directly or indirectly—from the dams. Many have also benefited from other project activities.

This project is unusual in that local people are few in number and are not a serious threat to local plants and animals. While the people's relationship with the project has generally been for employment, with limited participation in decisionmaking, the project appears to have made a promising start toward achieving its conservation goals.

Rwanda, Volcanoes National Park

Protected area. The 150 square kilometer Volcanoes National Park.

Project. Mountain Gorilla project.

Implementing organization. African Wildlife Foundation.

Responsible government agency. Rwandan Office of Tourism and Nature Protection.

Funding. A consortium of conservation organizations provides funding to the project. The lead organization is African Wildlife Foundation. Project budgets have increased from approximately

$50,000 a year at the outset project, to more than $250,000 a year in the late 1980s.

Project area and scope. Education activities focus on the Prefecture of Ruhengeri, which has a population of more than 500,000. An estimated 150,000 of these people live within 5 kilometers of the park. Most other project activities focus on the park itself.

Region. Rwanda's Mountain Gorilla project is one of the most celebrated conservation-development projects in Africa. The project has used tourism development to gain government and local support for conservation of the easternmost population of the African gorilla.

The project operates in Volcanoes National Park and protects a gorilla population shared by Rwanda, Uganda, and Zaire. The area surrounding the park is densely populated by low-income subsistence agriculturalists. Hunters living near the park engage in hunting practices that jeopardize the gorillas' survival. The park also has a history of having areas annexed for agricultural

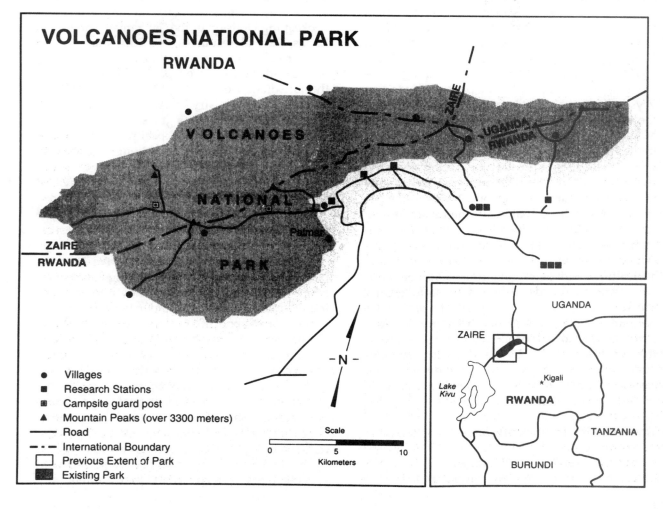

development schemes. In this setting the project evolved a strategy of gaining central government support for gorilla conservation through the development of tourism revenues and reducing local threats to the gorillas through improved enforcement and conservation education.

Project activities. Activities center on tourism development, conservation education, and law enforcement. Project staff habituated groups of gorillas to the presence of people, thus improving gorilla viewing and permitting increases in gorilla viewing fees. Visits increased from fewer than 2,000 people a year in 1979 to more than 6,000 in 1989, and revenues rose from a few thousand dollars annually to about a half million dollars a year. Project conservation education efforts have included village and school presentations and the use of posters, films, and radio. The project has a mobile education unit, two Rwandan educators, and a U.S. Peace Corps education volunteer. The project increased the park guard contingent from thirty to sixty, and has provided equipment and training for all guards.

Evaluation. The enormous growth in tourism revenues at Volcanoes National Park is almost wholly the result of the efforts of the Mountain Gorilla project. This growth in revenues brought about a dramatic improvement in central government and local support for the park. Attitude surveys indicate that most local farmers now support the continued existence of the park; before the Mountain Gorilla project, most favored converting the park to agriculture. Much of the change in attitude is due to a greater understanding of the watershed protection function of the park and its link to agricultural production. However, the potential for conflict remains. In the future, it may become increasingly difficult to reconcile the competing demands of the various groups with interests in the area: the desire of farmers for more agricultural land, of the government for more tourism and revenue, and of conservationists for greater protection of gorillas and the park. The project has not had a major grass-roots community development focus, and one of the interesting lessons of the project is that education and tourism development alone—without a strong rural development emphasis—can generate considerable local support for conservation.

Tanzania, East Usambara Mountains

Protected area. The East Usambara mountains in northern Tanzania belong to an old and isolated

mountain chain containing a high degree of biological endemism. Rainfall exceeds 2,000 millimeters a year and the mountains—with a high point of about 1,500 meters—are the main source of water for urban and agricultural areas in the adjacent lowlands. Topsoils are highly susceptible to erosion on the steep slopes. Industrial logging (until 1987), pit sawing, and undercropping of the canopy with cardamom have significantly degraded the natural forests, now limited to eighteen forest reserves (about 160 square kilometers) and 90 square kilometers of public land. Forest gaps have been extensively colonized by an exotic Maesopsis.

Project. The East Usambara Agricultural Development and Environmental Conservation project began in 1987. Finnida, the Finnish international development agency, conducted a separate forest inventory and prepared a management plan in 1988, which has not yet been implemented.

Implementing organizations. The Ministry of Agriculture and Livestock Development and the Tanga Regional Authorities, in collaboration with the International Union for Conservation of Nature and Natural Resources (IUCN) and the Forestry and Beekeeping Division of the Tanzanian Ministry of Lands, Natural Resources, and Tourism.

Responsible government agency. The forest reserves and the forests on public lands are under the jurisdiction of the Forestry and Beekeeping Division. The Ministry of Agriculture and Livestock Development has jurisdiction over the nonforested public lands. Local people also have rights over the public lands, although these rights are not clearly defined.

Funding. The European Community provided $1.5 million from February 1987 to June 1991.

Project area and scope. Based at Amani, the project has concentrated on fifteen villages near forest reserves in the southern East Usambara.

Region. Once-extensive forests have been replaced by a patchwork of shrinking forest remnants—many of them modified by human activity, tea estates, and smallholder farms. The local population of about 40,000 consists almost entirely of poor farmers from several tribes. Many are recent migrants attracted by wage labor opportunities in private coffee and, later, tea estates. Tea and cardamom, a major export crop encouraged by the government, are the area's principal crops. Cardamom requires shade from the natural forest canopy but degrades the soil after a few years of production, requiring the clearing of new areas.

Project activities. The project began in 1987 with staff seconded from government departments and

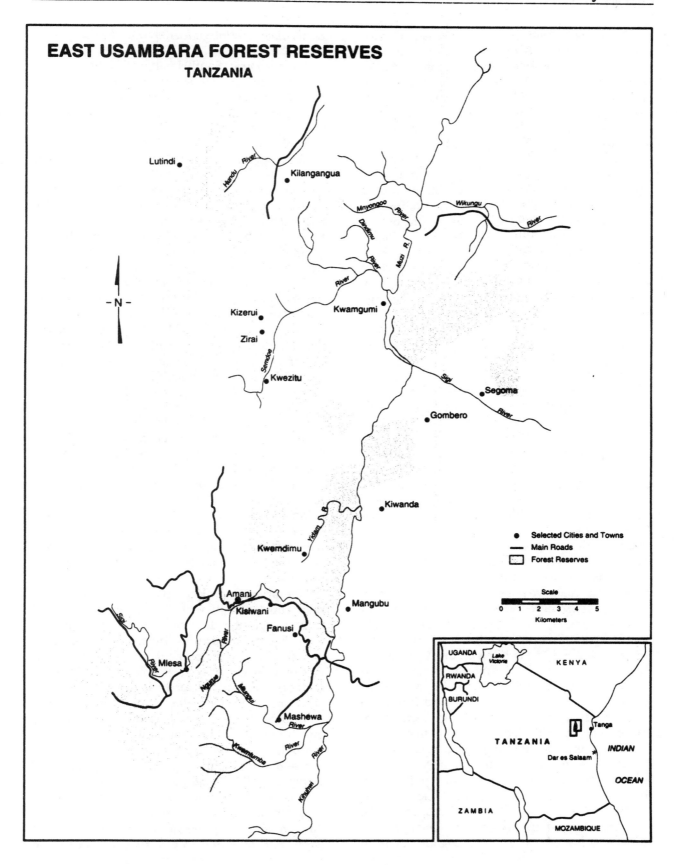

EAST USAMBARA FOREST RESERVES
TANZANIA

Lutindi

Kilangangua

Hardu River

Mnyongoo River

Dindimu River

Wikungu River

River

Muzi R.

Kizerui

Zirai

Semdoe River

Kwamgumi

Kwezitu

Sigi River

Segoma

Gombero

Kiwanda

Ydam R.

Kwemdimu

Amani

Kisiwani

Mangubu

Fanusi

Sigi River

Mlesa

Nguna River

Mkingu River

Mashewa
River

Kwamkumbe River

River

Kihuhwi River

Selected Cities and Towns

Main Roads

Forest Reserves

Scale

0 1 2 3 4 5
Kilometers

UGANDA   Lake Victoria   K E N Y A

RWANDA

BURUNDI

Tanga

T A N Z A N I A   INDIAN

Dar es Salaam   OCEAN

Z A M B I A

MOZAMBIQUE

two expatriate technical advisers. Village coordinators, one from each of fifteen villages, are employed as the project's extension agents. The government has guaranteed to continue these positions after the project ends. The project has promoted income-earning substitutes for cardamom that do not degrade the soils; encouraged contour planting; funded road repair and maintenance; hired villagers to plant 60 kilometers of boundary trees around the forest reserves; established private and village tree nurseries; and promoted small-scale cooperative enterprises, including fish ponds, pit sawing, and chicken raising. The project planned to extend its activities into villages throughout the East Usambara starting in 1990.

Evaluation. Implementation is at an early stage and difficult to evaluate. An effective community outreach mechanism was essential, given the large population and lengthy travel times between villages. The village coordinator approach seems to be working well, and project managers have won the respect of villagers and local government officials. A few farmers have begun growing trees and have adopted new cash crops, but there has been little progress in encouraging people to work together on cooperative income-generating ventures such as pit sawing. Community participation in project decisionmaking is limited. Prospects for sustainability are strengthened by the participation of government line agencies (the Ministry of Agriculture and Livestock Development and the Ministry of Land, Natural Resources, and Tourism), the placement of agency personnel in key project posts, and government guarantees of the village coordinator positions.

Adequate baseline surveys of the farming systems in the area have not been carried out. Further progress will require the widespread adoption of viable alternatives to cardamom. There is currently little evidence that project conservation goals are being achieved, although the ending of commercial logging in 1987 was critically important and the boundary tree planting was an important step in conserving the forest reserves. The forests on public lands, which deflect pressure from the reserves, continue to be degraded. Without strengthened enforcement, particularly to control pit sawing, it seems unlikely that the public land forests will survive for long, placing further pressure on the reserves. By late 1989 the project had achieved as much, if not more, than could reasonably be expected, although the predictions of financial self-sufficiency made by a 1985 planning mission from IUCN now seem unrealistic.

Zambia, Luangwa Integrated Rural Development Project

Protected area. South Luangwa National Park, 9,050 square kilometers; Lupande Game Management Area, 4,840 square kilometers.

Project. Luangwa Integrated Rural Development project (LIRDP).

Implementing organization. The government of Zambia, special regional authority specific to the project.

Responsible government agency. The project is ultimately responsible to an interministerial committee chaired by the president of Zambia. Routine project direction is provided by an advisory committee housed in the National Commission on Development Planning.

Funding. Funding is primarily by NORAD, the development agency of the Norwegian government. The five-year NORAD grant is for $25 million.

Project area and scope. The project encompasses all of South Luangwa National Park and the Lupande Game Management Area, where the population totals about 35,000.

Project activities. The Luangwa Integrated Rural Development project (LIRDP) was initiated by the government of Zambia in 1986, although full-scale implementation did not begin until 1988. The project is a coordinating umbrella for all government action in the valley. Project oversight includes antipoaching, road construction and maintenance, agricultural extension, forestry and fisheries development, and wildlife use. Project activities are supported in the short term by donor contributions and in the long term by a revolving fund that accumulates revenues from resource development in the valley.

The primary project development initiative is road construction, while antipoaching law enforcement is the dominant conservation investment. Since a major impediment to antipoaching and economic development in the valley is the lack of all-season roads, over half of the project's budget is devoted to road maintenance and improvement. Project plans call for hiring and equipping 300 game scouts by 1992. Roughly one-third of these scouts will be provided through the village scout program. Salary, training, and equipment for guards amount to about 10 percent of the total project budget. Coordination of the diverse government programs that the project directs requires a major investment in administration. The project has two directors and a large staff dedicated to ensuring integrated and sustainable development of the valley. Project activities are supported by revenues from development of a diverse set of renewable natural resources through a revolving fund. Forty percent of fund revenues are allocated to community projects while 60 percent go to project management costs, including the village scout program and road improvement. Revenues from wildlife use are the greatest contributor to the revolving fund, but forestry concession fees may be important in the future.

Evaluation (see Kiss 1990). It is too early to draw conclusions from the experience of the project, which is diverse and ambitious and depends in large measure on the unique management skills of its two directors. Development progress under the project will come from improved access to markets, and through improved coordination of government development programs. The project is similar to Lupande/ADMADE in some ways. It has a greater capacity to collect fees from diverse sources and to spend them. However, the link between maintenance of wildlife populations and dispersed regional development activities is less clear than in ADMADE. The degree to which a regional bureaucratic authority can improve the responsiveness of government programs to local needs is the key issue for LIRDP.

Zambia, South Luangwa National Park

Protected area. South Luangwa National Park, 9,050 square kilometers; Lupande Game Management Area, 4,840 square kilometers.

Project. Lupande Development project and ADMADE.

Implementing agency and responsible government agency. The government of Zambia, and the National Parks and Wildlife Services.

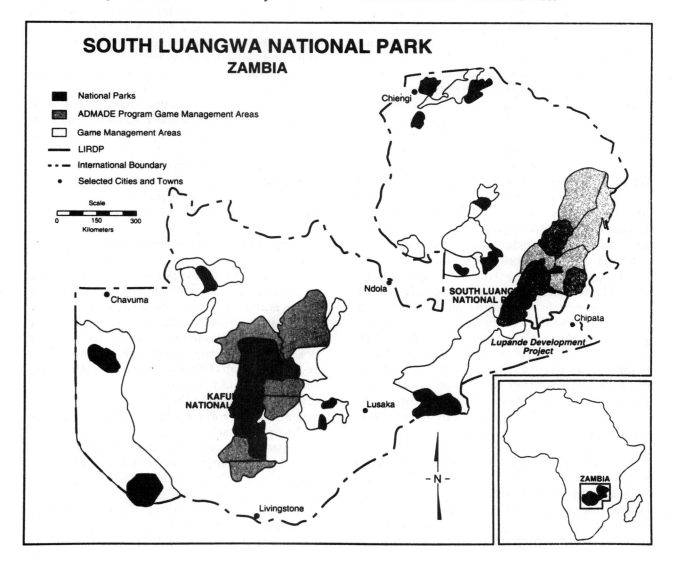

SOUTH LUANGWA NATIONAL PARK
ZAMBIA

- ■ National Parks
- ▨ ADMADE Program Game Management Areas
- □ Game Management Areas
- —— LIRDP
- – – – International Boundary
- • Selected Cities and Towns

Scale
0   150   300
Kilometers

Chiengi

Ndola

SOUTH LUANGWA
NATIONAL PARK

Chipata

Lupande Development
Project

Chavuma

KAFUE
NATIONAL PARK

Lusaka

Livingstone

– N –

ZAMBIA

Funding. Several donors have funded various program components. The largest single donor has been the World Wildlife Fund. Project budgets for activities at Lupande—exclusive of national expansion—have averaged about $50,000 a year.

Project area and scope. The Lupande project addresses a community of 400 to 500 people in the Malama area of the Lupande Game Management Area, which covers approximately 400 square kilometers.

Region. The Lupande Development project is in a game management area next to Zambia's South Luangwa National Park. Safari hunting is permitted in the game management area, as are human habitation and subsistence use of wildlife. The value of wildlife in the area is high, and one purpose of the project is to return some of this value to the communities that bear the costs of living with wildlife.

Economic activity in the Lupande area is extremely limited. Infrastructure is poor, roads are impassable through much of the rainy season, and there are few opportunities for formal sector employment. Villages in the area engage in subsistence agriculture, which is constrained by the presence of the Tsetse and crop damage by wildlife.

Project activities. Project activities were initiated in 1985 and have been supported by several donors. The main activities are a wildlife harvesting program, the return of hunting fee revenues to local communities, a wildlife harvesting program, and the hiring and training of local game scouts (the village scout program). The keystone of the Lupande approach is a policy change that allows revenues from safari hunting concessions to be returned to local villages. These revenues are applied to local development initiatives at the discretion of local chiefs. A second important feature of the Lupande project is the community harvest and processing of wildlife. Harvesting focuses on hippopotamus, the skins and meat of which are marketed inside Zambia. Revenue from this program is lower than from revenue returns, but employment generation is high, which is of major significance in the Lupande area.

Part of the revenues from safari hunting and wildlife harvest are used to hire supplementary game scouts from local villages. These village scouts are trained and equipped by the project and patrol their home areas.

Evaluation (see Kiss 1990). Revenue return and employment have generated powerful incentives for communities in the Lupande area to value wildlife. This is evidenced in strong community support for the village scout program, where villagers had previously been strongly antagonistic to government wildlife personnel. Early evidence from the project indicates dramatic reductions in poaching levels in the Lupande game management area and in adjacent areas of South Luangwa National Park.

The Lupande approach was replicated as ADMADE in more than ten other game management areas in Zambia beginning in 1987. ADMADE expands on many of the elements of the Lupande project. Game management areas (GMAS) are divided into administrative wildlife management units. The project's goal is for these units to support their own wildlife management costs and to generate funds for community projects. A revolving fund returns 35 percent of revenues from safari and other hunting fees to community projects within the GMA, 40 percent to wildlife management activities withihn the GMA, including the village scout program, 15 percent to the national park system, and 10 percent to the Zambian Tourist Bureau. The link between wildlife populations and community revenue is clearly established in the ADMADE program. Reductions in poaching have been substantial thus far, and local employment has been high. However, community involvement in decisionmaking and the distribution of local benefits has not been widely participatory at the local level. Still, the project represents an important example of linking wildlife management to community development.

Asia

Indonesia, Dumoga-Bone National Park

Protected area. Dumoga-Bone National Park is the most important conservation area in northern Sulawesi and ranks as one of the highest conservation priorities in Southeast Asia. The 3,000 square kilometer park consists primarily of closed-canopy rain forest among rugged mountains reaching 2,000 meters. The central Bulawan mountain range runs north-south, and two major rivers flow from the park boundaries—the Dumoga to the east and the Bone to the west. The establishment of the park in 1982-84 was closely linked with the development of two irrigation projects in the Dumoga valley.

Projects. The Kosinggolan and Toraut irrigation projects in the Dumoga valley, allowing farmers to grow paddy rice.

Implementing organizations. Various ministries of the government of Indonesia, the government of North Sulawesi, and the World Bank.

Responsible government agency. The Directorate General for Forest Protection and Nature Conservation in the Ministry of Forests.

Funding. A $60 million World Bank loan (Irrigation XV).

Project area and scope. The eastern regions of the park protect the upper watershed of the Dumoga river, which irrigates 110 square kilometers of rice fields cultivated by 8,500 farmers—mainly migrants and transmigrants.

Region. In 1960, the population of the fertile 300 square kilometer Dumoga valley was about 8,000. By 1980, migrants and transmigrants had increased this number to almost 50,000. This rapid expansion—linked with improved road access, land speculation, absentee landlords, and traditional agricultural practices—contributed to increasing pressure on the region's forests. The existing Kosinggolan irrigation scheme was only partly functional in 1980, and interruptions in the water supply were attributed to deforestation of the catchment area. The World Bank was asked for a loan to complete the Kosingollan scheme and develop the Toraut scheme.

Project activities. Disbursements from the loan were conditional upon the government halting deforestation of the catchment areas, to ensure a con-stant water supply for irrigation. This was achieved through strict enforcement, and the national park was established in 1982. More than 400 farmers were evicted from the park in 1983, and each family was provided with about 2 hectares and a house. The estimated resettlement cost was 1.1 million rupiah per family, or about $240,000 overall. The Kosinggolan scheme was completed in 1984, irrigating 4,400 hectares and benefiting 3,700 farmers. Construction included 56 kilometers of main and secondary canals, 259 kilometers of tertiary and quaternary canals, and 258 kilometers of inspection roads. During the following six years, average farmer incomes and production levels doubled or tripled. The Toraut scheme was completed in 1988, irrigating 6,600 hectares and benefiting 4,800 farmers. Construction included 56 kilometers of main and secondary canals, 330 kilometers of tertiary and quaternary canals, and 355 kilometers of inspection roads.

Evaluation. This project demonstrates how a strong linkage can be established between effective park management and local economies in a situation where watershed protection is critical for adjacent agriculture. Several factors contributed to project success. Data collected on illegal settlers provided an important input to resettlement plans

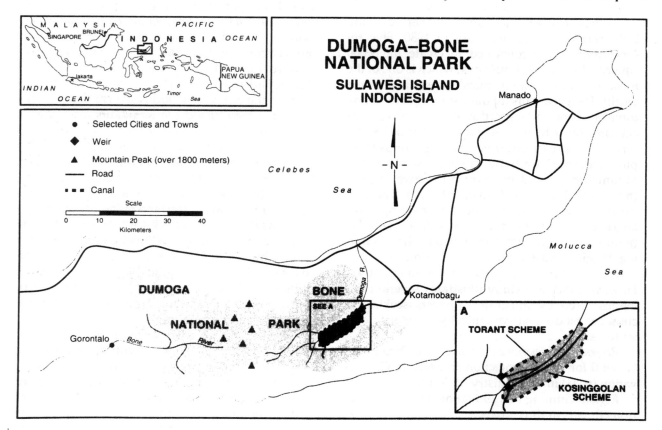

and law enforcement action. The provincial government played a highly supportive role and continues to cooperate effectively with the park management. The loan funds included substantial budgets for park guard patrols and extension programs by local government representatives. And forest concessions at the park borders were canceled.

Some of the original Dumoga valley inhabitants were adversely affected. Being accustomed to dryland agriculture and the periodic clearance of forest for new land, they did not adapt rapidly to the more intensive and profitable irrigated rice cultivation. While some were forced to sell their land, others sold theirs voluntarily at low prices and then attempted unsuccessfully to reenter the protected forest.

Effective enforcement against landless migrants and, more recently, gold prospectors has been the principal approach to protecting the park. The immigrant wet-rice farmers pose little threat to the park because they have no interest in clearing forest land and presumably receive enough income to make poaching unattractive. The original Dumoga inhabitants have inadvertently been dispersed and no longer threaten the park.

Indonesia, Gunung Leuser National Park

Protected area. Gunung Leuser became Indonesia's first national park in 1980. Five reserve areas were combined to create the 9,000 square kilometer national park, which is one of the most important tropical moist forest areas in the world. The park is one of the last refuges for many threatened and endangered species requiring tropical rain forest habitat. A wide variety of habitat types are represented, from coastal swamps to alpine vegetation on Sumatra's highest mountain. Mountainous areas predominate, however, and there are relatively few lowland areas. The species-rich lowlands tend to be the most important areas for conserving biodiversity. They are also the areas most seriously threatened by illegal hunting, logging and agricultural expansion.

Project. There is no project at Gunung Leuser. However, the case study illustrates several challenges faced by integrated projects seeking to conserve biodiversity in critically threatened ecosystems.

Responsible government agency. The Directorate General for Forest Protection and Nature Conservation (PHPA) in the Ministry of Forests.

Region. Gunung Leuser National Park faces serious threats in three areas:

- The park is now bisected by the Kutacane-Blangkejeren road, which was improved in the early 1980s, with USAID funding. As a result of the improved access, the park's lowland forests within 1 to 5 kilometers of the road, which contain the greatest biological diversity, are being severely degraded by illegal logging and agricultural encroachment, particularly in the area of three rapidly expanding enclaves. Long-term ecological studies at the world-renowned Ketambe Research Forest may have to be abandoned because of illegal logging.
- Lowland forests inside the park on the lower slopes of the Alas river valley are being logged and replaced by dryland smallholder farming.
- Encroachment and logging at several points on the outer park boundary are increasing.

The extensive logging and agriculture in the park is occurring even on very steep slopes. Illegal logging trails, poorly draining roadsides, and denuded hillsides have all contributed to increasing soil erosion, landslides, heavy silt loads in rivers, and floods following heavy rains. Illegal activity is obvious from the road, with no attempt at concealment. Firewood is sold at the roadside, and no enforcement of park regulations is evident. National park personnel appear to have had no effect on the rate of forest destruction. Although the personnel are underequipped and understaffed, the critical constraint appears to be local resentment toward the park, at village and higher political levels. Park officials who have reported illegal practices to the police or to local government authorities have been subject to intimidation and threats. This situation has been documented and reported several times in the last decade.

Lack of local support for the park is understandable in Aceh Tenggara District, where 82 percent of the land has been set aside for conservation. Virtually all of the land suitable for agriculture has already been colonized, much of it in the park, and the expanding population may have little choice but to clear more forest. Any new initiatives to safeguard the park would appear doomed without a fundamental shift in the relationship between the park and the Aceh Tenggara government and local communities.

The Indonesian government is unlikely to support more rigorous enforcement measures in the politically sensitive Aceh region; however, there are at least two sites outside the national park boundaries that appear to have the potential for the development of irrigated agriculture. These

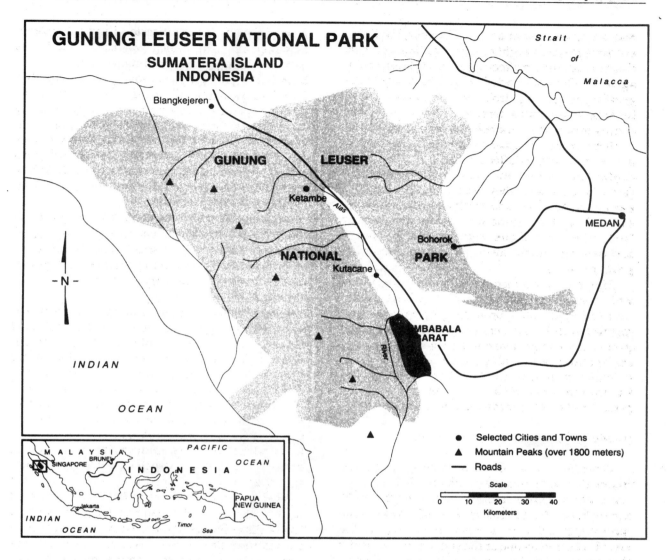

GUNUNG LEUSER NATIONAL PARK
SUMATERA ISLAND
INDONESIA

Blangkejeren

GUNUNG   LEUSER

Ketambe

Alas

NATIONAL

Kutacane

Bohorok   PARK

MEDAN

MBABALA
BARAT

River

Strait

of

Malacca

INDIAN

OCEAN

● Selected Cities and Towns
▲ Mountain Peaks (over 1800 meters)
— Roads

Scale

0   10   20   30   40
Kilometers

MALAYSIA
SINGAPORE   BRUNEI
INDONESIA
Jakarta
INDIAN
OCEAN   Timor   Sea

PACIFIC
OCEAN

PAPUA
NEW GUINEA

may offer an opportunity for an integrated approach to development that can conserve the park. Gunung Leuser is one of several parks included in World Bank-funded forestry projects. This may provide an opportunity for a fresh look at this difficult situation.

Nepal, Annapurna Conservation Area

Protected area. The 2,600 square kilometer **Annapurna Conservation Area** is arguably the most geographically and culturally diverse conservation area in the world. There is a unique mix of ecosystems, mostly unaltered by human activity, including subtropical lowland, high alpine meadows, desert plateaus, and oak, rhododendron and bamboo forests. The world's deepest river gorge and some of the highest mountains are located here. The Annapurna Sanctuary near the center of the conservation area is a natural amphitheater surrounded by several peaks of more than 6,700 meters. The wet southern slopes support a rich variety of birds and mammals, including Danfe pheasant, Himalayan tahr, barking deer, serow, goral, Himalayan black bear, musk deer, and the rare red panda. The dry northern slopes, which extend to the Tibetan border, contain snow leopard and blue sheep.

Project. The Annapurna Conservation Area project.

Implementing organization. The King Mahendra Trust for Nature Conservation (KMTNC), Nepal's largest conservation organization, established in 1983.

Responsible government agency. The government of Nepal, which has delegated its authority to KMTNC.

Funding. First phase (1986-89): $440,000, including $351,000 from the World Wildlife Fund (WWF) and $85,000 from the U.K. trust of the KMTNC; second phase (1989-93): the total project revenue from all sources from 1989 to the present is about $200,000 a year.

Project area and scope. The first phase (1986-89) concentrated on 800 square kilometers of the southern slopes. An 1,800 square kilometer extension began in 1990.

Region. About 40,000 people of diverse ethnic backgrounds inhabit the Annapurna area, where agriculture and trade have flourished for hundreds of years in the steep-sided Himalayan valleys. Most of the people are poor rural farmers. More than 30,000 foreign trekkers visit the area each year, leading to a proliferation of small tea shops and lodges along the trails. During the last two decades, large areas of forested land have been cleared for use in cooking and heating for visitors. Expanding agriculture, water pollution, poor sanita-

tion, and littering on trekking routes have all accelerated, as has the rapid expansion of the resident population. These conditions led to a royal directive in 1985 to improve tourist development while safeguarding the environment. The KMTNC conducted surveys that led to new legislation establishing the Annapurna Conservation Area in 1986, specifically allowing hunting, collection of forest products, use of visitor fees for local development, and the delegation of management authority to the village level.

Project activities. The project objective is to help the inhabitants—particularly the region's poor farmers—maintain control over their environment. The area is split into zones that permit varying degrees of protection and land use. A headquarters was established in Ghandruk, the intensive use zone, with a mainly local staff. Activities have included community development, forest management, conservation education, research, and train-

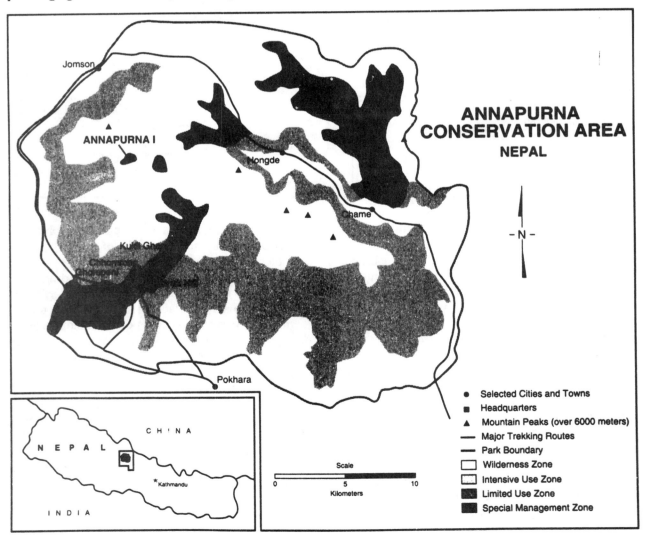

ing. High priority was given to reducing the environmental effects of visiting trekkers and increasing the local economic benefits from tourism. Entry fees generate 4 million rupee ($160,000) annually for the project. Training courses for lodge-owners helped upgrade the quality of service, standardize menus and prices, and improve standards of sanitation and waste disposal. Lodges and expeditions were required to use kerosene inside the conservation area; fuelwood is for subsistence use only. Reviving a traditional organization structure, a forest management committee was established in Ghandruk to enforce regulations (fining poachers, controlling timber cutting).

Evaluation. The project started with four important advantages: (1) the monarchy's personal interest; (2) specific supporting legislation; (3) the autonomy granted to KMTNC; and (4) field surveys and discussions with local people preceding establishment of the conservation area. The kerosene regulation has substantially reduced deforestation rates, and training programs have reduced the harmful effects of tourism and improved the livelihoods of lodgeowners. However, the significant economic benefits from tourism have not been distributed widely. There is little evidence to suggest that most poor farmers will benefit from the project. The project has made progress in motivating a skeptical local population to make some forest management decisions, although local institutions are not likely to assume major responsibility for several years. The project's capable and well-organized staff have established a solid foundation for future expansion; to label the project an unambiguous success, however, would be premature. Collection of fees from visitors will contribute valuable revenues to the project, but original forecasts of financial self-sufficiency by 1993 appear optimistic.

Nepal, Royal Chitwan National Park

Protected area. Royal Chitwan National Park is in the subtropical Terai region of Nepal. Chitwan had been protected as a royal hunting reserve from 1846 to the early 1950s but was not made a national park until 1973. The original protected area of 544 square kilometers was extended to 932 square kilometers in 1977 and designated as a World Heritage Site by UNESCO in 1982. Vegetation is dominated by Sal forests and the world's tallest grasses, reaching 5 to 7 meters. Grasslands occupy about 20 percent of the park, supporting one of the most impressive assemblages of large mammals in Asia. The park is one of the last remaining habitats of the one-horned Asian rhinoceros and the Bengal tiger. Chitwan also contains wild boar, gaur, four species of deer, and the greatest diversity of birds of any park in Nepal. The number of large mammals, which had been declining, has increased dramatically since the park was established and hunting was strictly controlled. The Nepalese army provides more than 500 armed guards for law enforcement, funded from the national park budget. The first wildlife safari lodge was established in 1965, and the park is now a popular tourist destination. Seven high-cost tourist lodges are licensed to operate inside the park and more than forty small ones have sprung up outside.

Project. There is no formal project in the park, but once a year villagers are permitted to collect tall grasses for house construction and thatching from the park, the only remaining local source.

Responsible government agency. Department of National Parks and Wildlife Conservation.

Funding. The grass collection activities have not received outside funding.

Project area and scope. More than 100,000 people from local villages take part in the grass collection.

Region. The Terai was largely unpopulated until malaria eradication programs began to open up the fertile plains to agriculture in the 1950s. Rice, maize, wheat, and mustard are the major crops. Extensive immigration from the hills then led to massive conversion of the Terai forests to agricultural land. Population doubled during the 1970s, and about 260,000 people occupied 320 villages around the park boundary in 1980; the population continues to grow at about 6 percent annually. Many of the communities close to the park boundaries lack fuelwood and grazing land. For generations, local people had used the park area to collect fuelwood, graze livestock, and collect tall grasses for construction. The forced relocation of several villages from inside the proposed park area generated considerable local hostility and mistrust. Since the establishment of the park, further tension and conflict have arisen because of prohibitions on grazing and collection of forest products, and because of human injury and death as well as crop and livestock loss from large mammals protected in the park. Enforcement is strict: during 1985, for example, 554 people were fined and 1,306 livestock impounded. Initial hopes that tourism would provide significant local benefits now appear unfounded, because most local people have little direct involvement with tourist activities.

Project activities. Although there is no formal

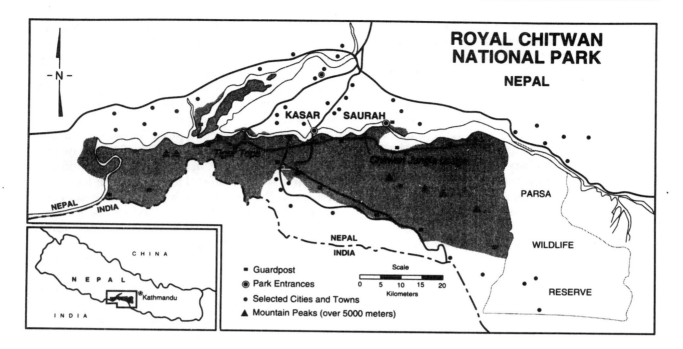

ROYAL CHITWAN NATIONAL PARK

NEPAL

■ Guardpost
◉ Park Entrances
• Selected Cities and Towns
▲ Mountain Peaks (over 5000 meters)

project, once a year villagers are permitted to collect tall grasses for house construction and thatching from the park. This grass cutting is not considered detrimental to wildlife because it is permitted only at the end of the growing season when most plant material is dead, of poor nutritional quality, and unattractive as food for wildlife. A 1986-87 study estimated that roughly 11 million kilograms of grass products were collected, valued at 10 million rupees ($450,000). Subtracting permit costs and imputed labor costs yields a net value to the local economy of about 5.5 million rupees ($250,000), which is roughly equivalent to the annual budget of the park. Fifty-seven percent of the grass cutters had walked 3-6 kilometers to the park, and an additional 32 percent had come 10-16 kilometers. Cutters were asked what they liked about the park. Thatch grass collection scored highest. Firewood collection, an illegal activity, ranked second. The study found that there are few locally available alternatives to thatching grass for roofing—none of them affordable to the villagers. The local fuelwood deficiency is serious, and illegal collection during the grass-cutting season is a threat to the future of the grass program. Park authorities have estimated that the amount of firewood taken from the park during grass-cutting equals or exceeds the value of all grass materials removed.

Evaluation. Except for grass collection, the benefits flowing from the park to local people are minor because most local people are not directly involved in tourism. Although the benefits of the

grass program are substantial, overall the park imposes considerable hardship on local communities. The people appear to have little choice but to continue illegally taking their cattle into the park and collecting fuelwood. Pressure on the park will increase unless alternatives can be found. Without the presence of the Nepalese army, it seems unlikely that Chitwan would have survived to the present.

Thailand, Khao Yai National Park

Protected area. The 2,200 square kilometer Khao Yai National Park is located about 200 kilometers northeast of Bangkok. It includes some of the largest remaining areas of tropical moist forest in mainland Asia, and contains exceptionally diverse flora and fauna. It has been described as the highest priority site for plant conservation in Thailand, and for many rare animal species, it is one of the last remaining viable habitats in Thailand. Khao Yai attracts 250,000 to 400,000 Thai and foreign visitors annually who spend 100 million to 200 million baht ($4-8 million) on admission, lodging fees, transportation, food, and other services in the park.

Projects. The Sup Tai Rural Development for Conservation project and the Environmental Awareness and Development Mobilization (TEAM) project.

Implementing organizations. The Population and Community Development Association (PDA), the largest nongovernmental organization in Thailand with community development experience in 16,000 villages, and Wildlife Fund Thailand (WFT), a small but increasingly influential nongovernmental organization affiliated with the World Wildlife Fund-International (WWF).

Responsible government agency. National Parks Division of the Royal Forest Department.

Funding. For the Sup Tai project (1985-90), Agro Action (a German foundation) provided 5 million baht ($200,000), and PDA one million baht ($40,000). For the TEAM project, USAID provided WFT with a three-year grant for the TEAM project of 5.3 million baht ($212,000).

Project area and scope. About 150 villages surround Khao Yai. The PDA and WFT began a project at Sup Tai village in 1985. In 1987 WFT withdrew from Sup Tai and initiated the TEAM project in ten villages, with conservation education activities in another forty villages. PDA expanded into two villages close to Sup Tai in 1987 and planned to extend into three more in 1990.

Region. About 53,000 people live in 150 villages just outside the park boundaries. Most illegally occupy "reserved forest" (as do more than 7 mil-

lion Thai villagers). Enforcement has resulted in hostility and armed clashes between park personnel and local villagers, with loss of life on both sides, but illegal activities—poaching and the removal of timber—in the park continue. Recognizing the need to address local concerns, the PDA and WFT began to work together on the park boundaries. Initial surveys revealed that middlemen (loan sharks) controlled village economies, providing credit to farmers at 5 percent a month and then taking over the lands of those unable to make repayments. The debt situation of villagers was identified as the major constraint to change.

Project activities. The Sup Tai project was based upon a village environmental protection society. An elected village committee administers the environmental protection society with supervision from a full-time PDA project manager. The project provides low-interest loans to the environmental protection society members from a revolving loan fund in exchange for promises not to break park regulations. Wildlife Fund Thailand's TEAM project and the PDA's expansion into more villages are based on the Sup Tai model. Project activities at the target villages have included park trekking for tour-

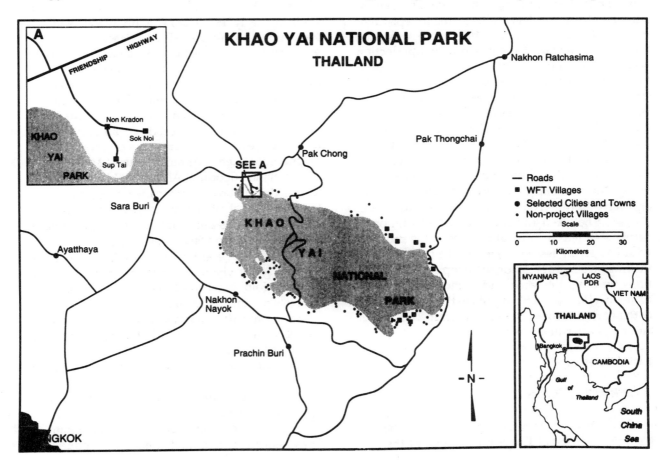

ists, cooperative stores, community forestry, environmental education, park boundary tree planting, agricultural extension, and training village health volunteers. Sup Tai village also benefited from a new road to Bankok and electrification of the village—both indirect benefits of the project, which neither funded nor instigated the changes.

Evaluation. Villagers and officials assert that illegal activities are continuing throughout the park, principally hunting and logging, although the projects have led to improved relations between villagers and park personnel. Clarification of the park boundaries around Sup Tai eliminated much confusion and ended agricultural encroachment near the village. The new road and the provision of electricity to Sup Tai are both regarded as significant economic benefits by villagers, although the resulting increase in land prices threatens the landless. Many Sup Tai farmers have sold their land. Others have lost their lands to creditors, joining Thailand's growing landless population. The effect on the park of rapidly changing land ownership patterns cannot be predicted.

The environmental protection society loan programs are the most important economic benefits from the projects, although the scale has been insufficient for the villagers to become independent of the middlemen. By late 1989 there was little prospect of the Sup Tai environmental protection society becoming self-sufficient in the near future. Other direct economic benefits flowing from the projects are more difficult to measure. Farming practices that emphasize soil conservation and new crop varieties have had some success, mainly in Sup Tai, but even there adoption has not been widespread. Project personnel are capable, dedicated, and highly respected by the villagers, although the TEAM approach of two project managers each covering five villages appears inadequate. The split between the PDA and WFT has unfortunately resulted in a loss of balance in the projects, with PDA giving less emphasis to the park and WFT making little progress on development. Evaluations by PDA's Research and Evaluation Division have provided valuable inputs to the management of the various projects, but even in Sup Tai, project successes are still elusive.

Latin America

Costa Rica, Osa Peninsula

Protected area. The Osa Peninsula, in the extreme southwest of Costa Rica, is one of the few lowland tropical forests intact in Central America. Much of the 1,750 square kilometer peninsula is protected; it includes the Corcovado National Park, the Golfo Dulce Forest Reserve, the Guaymi Indigenous Reserve, Isla de Cano Biological Reserve, and the Golfito Forest Reserve.

Project. Boscosa project.

Implementing organization. The Conservation Foundation (affiliated with the World Wildlife Fund) designed and raised funds for the project. It is administered in Costa Rica through the Fundacion Neotropica.

Responsible government agency. Several government agencies are involved. The National Parks Service (parks and biological reserves); Forestry Directorate (forest reserves); National Commission on Indigenous Affairs (Indian reservations); and the Conservation Unit in the Ministry of Mines, Energy, and Natural Resources.

Funding. Approximately $350,000 from various sources for 1988-91.

Project area and scope. Boscosa is a pilot project, initiated in December 1987, to "maintain forest cover on the Osa Peninsula, including Corcovado National Park and surrounding buffer zones."

Region. Limited access protected the peninsula until the early 1960s. Now, Corcovado National Park and the Golfo Dulce Forest Reserve are threatened by farmers practicing slash-and-burn agriculture, uncontrolled hunting, small-scale timber extraction, and small to medium-size gold mining. These problems have been exacerbated by the withdrawal of a banana company, which put thousands out of work. Deforestation had been limited to a flat area, but is increasing on steep slopes, destroying watersheds and increasing soil erosion and lowlands flooding. Although this rampant resource destruction is occurring to assure subsistence, the level of living for many is declining. Agricultural soils are rapidly losing productivity, timber and gold revenues earn little on the peninsula, and there is little to reinvest. Government services generally have been low. Confrontation between gold miners and park staff have escalated to levels of personal injury.

Project activities. Boscosa is a pilot project that has been in operation for a little more than two years. The original focus on forestry activities has expanded to deal with the complex socioeconomic problems of the region. Activities include natural forest management, improved agriculture and agroforestry, reforestation, and ecotourism. These activities were devised after an extensive planning phase—including socioeconomic surveys and land tenure, land use, and land capacity studies—was conducted in one community that has served as the focus for numerous project components. From this community, the project has recently branched into other areas. Boscosa's strategy has been to help create or support local organizations that can implement project activities and to work with local communities in a process they call "participative community extension." In addition to work at the community level, Boscosa is facilitating the preparation of a regional development plan for the peninsula, in consultation with government and local institutions.

Evaluation. The Boscosa project has achieved a great deal in a relatively short time. The project has been well funded and has been implemented by two collaborating nongovernmental organizations with support from the government. Substantial attention to information gathering and local participation in the design phase has proved its value in project implementation. The project has expanded from working with one community to working with twelve local organizations on the peninsula on natural forest management activities covering more than 8 square kilometers. More than 1.7 square kilometers have been reforested with

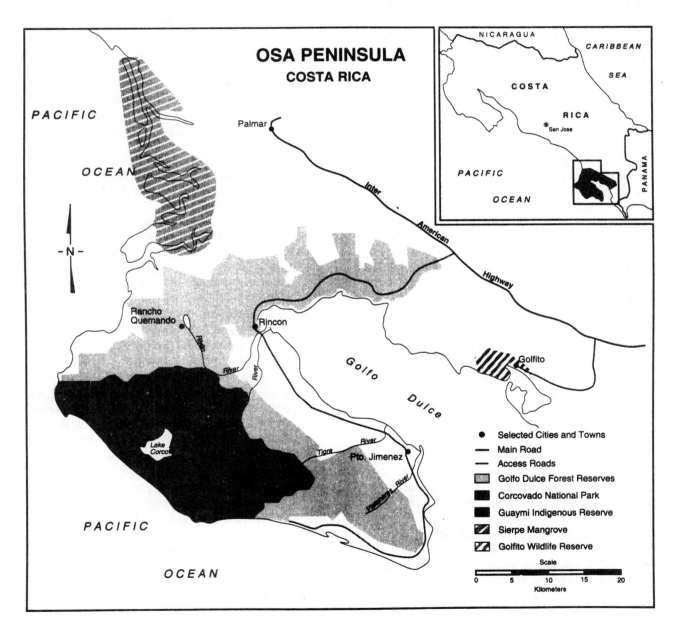

native species. The project has initiated policy dialogue with the government to improve coordination of government activities on the Osa Peninsula. The government established a system of conservation areas to integrate conservation and development throughout the country (based to a large extent on the Boscosa experience). The project has numerous other components that appear to be highly successful, although it is difficult to measure their impact. Despite its many successes over a relatively short period, there is little evidence thus far that the project has reduced illegal patterns of logging in the forest reserves or encroachment into the park. However, the achievements of this "pilot" project and the approaches developed to date are of considerable importance to the future design of ICDPs.

Costa Rica, Talamanca Region

Protected area. The Talamanca region contains two national parks, one biological reserve, one protected zone, five indigenous reservations, and one wildlife refuge spanning diverse ecosystems—beaches, coastal plains, mangroves, and tropical moist forest. The Gandoca-Manzanillo Wildlife Refuge has 50 square kilometers of contiguous private landholdings, some under cultivation and others wild, 44 square kilometers of marine areas, and a 60 square kilometer buffer zone between the refuge and intensively used agricultural areas. Endangered species found in the refuge include manatees, caimans, crocodiles, and tapirs. La Amistad Biosphere Reserve covers more than 2,000 square kilometers.

Project. ANAI Talamanca project.

Implementing agency. ANAI was founded in 1976 to "integrate conservation of natural ecosystems with the development needs of rural peoples." It works exclusively in the Talamanca region.

Responsible government agency. Numerous government agencies have jurisdiction: National Parks Service (parks and biological reserves); Forestry Directorate (forest reserves); Wildlife Office (wildlife refuges); National Commission on Indigenous Affairs (indigenous reservations); and the Conservation Unit in the Ministry of Mines, Energy, and Natural Resources (La Amistad Biosphere Reserve).

Funding. ANAI has received over $1.5 million since 1984, including support from a variety of foundations and nongovernmental organizations and Dutch debt-swap funds.

Project area and scope. The Talamanca region of Costa Rica comprises virtually all of the southeastern portion of the country. ANAI initiated activities there in 1976. The primary focus of project activities is the Gandoca-Manzanillo Wildlife Refuge and the adjacent La Amistad Biosphere Reserve.

Region. The Talamanca region is one of the most racially heterogeneous zones in Costa Rica, with blacks, mestizos (mixed Spaniards and Indians), and Indians. Most are small-scale farmers and many grow cacao as their primary cash crop. Timber extraction and commercial banana plantations also provide employment. The reliance on forest resources is strongly related to external factors such as timber and cacao prices and employment opportunities with the banana companies. Resource exploitation is more intense when cacao production or prices fall or when companies lay off workers. Cacao prices and employment have been major problems in recent years. Road construction into the area has led to high in-migration, increased tourism, land speculation, and deforestation. Migrants and timber contractors have increasingly cleared forest land.

Project activities. The ANAI philosophy is to promote land stewardship and individual responsibility as much as possible. The initial focal point for project activities was the Gandoca-Manzanillo area. Since about 1987, however, project activities have increasingly become widespread throughout Talamanca. ANAI helped twenty-four communities in Talamanca develop self-supporting tree nurseries and is training a representative from each community in agriculture and forestry. A land titling program for farmers in or near the refuge was initiated in the mid-1980s. The project is also working with groups of farmers to maintain sections of their farms in forests, sponsoring several small research projects on wildlife and natural resources, and taking responsibility for the creation of the refuge and assisting with its management and protection. ANAI helped establish a cacao marketing association and has initiated numerous pilot projects, ranging from iguana ranching to butterfly collecting.

Evaluation. ANAI has made progress in establishing self-sustaining community nurseries, which have produced more than 1.8 million trees, and in creating an official wildlife refuge. Their agroforestry activities may have increased household income and land use by improving cacao production—but few records are kept, making evaluation difficult. Other activities are too recent in origin to show any clear results linking conservation and development. The area ANAI works in is

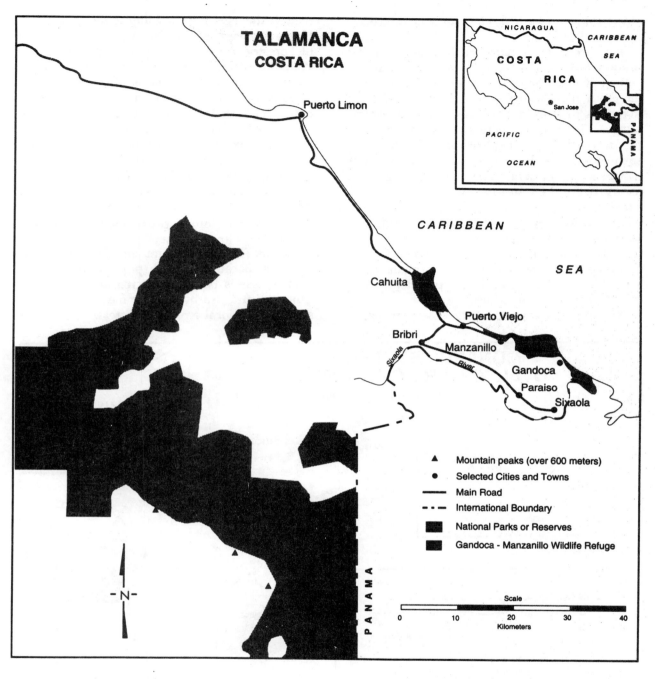

huge, and ANAI has several activities under way; thus, the activities are too dispersed to have significant conservation or development effects. Activities are not based on a project cycle or plan, but are initiated as funds and staffing permit. As yet, no significant local organizations have been created—apart from the recently established cacao marketing association—and no formal process has been initiated to involve local people in project decision-making.

As a nongovernmental organization, ANAI has a relatively low profile and seeks only to improve the situation in the Talamanca region. Principally because of the municipality's interest in unrestrained growth, ANAI has been unable to get local government support. However, it has succeeded in convincing government officials of the need to link development and conservation and to provide local people with benefits. To date, the breadth of the activities, coupled with rapid regional changes, has prevented ANAI from clearly demonstrating how this can be done.

Mexico, Monarch Butterfly Overwintering Reserves

Protected area. Estimates are that more than 100 million Monarch butterflies migrate from the United States and Canada to Mexico for the winter. From mid-November to mid-March, they rest in oyamel fir trees in the volcanic range of central Mexico. Five reserves were established to protect the overwintering habitat of the butterflies—4.5 square kilometers in reserves and 116 square kilometers in buffer areas. The volcanic range also forms part of the watershed for Mexico City and surrounding cities.

Project. Monarch Butterfly Overwintering Reserve Protection.

Implementing organization. Monarca, A.C. is a private Mexican nongovernmental organization established in 1980, following a presidential decree to protect the butterflies.

Responsible government agency. Reserve manage-ment is the legal responsibility of the Ministry of Urban Development and Ecology. The Subministry of Forestry, in the Ministry of Agriculture and Water Resources, is responsible for forest management and tree health and harvesting.

Funding. Funding for Monarca, A.C. and its activities for 1985-90 has exceeded $250,000, most of it provided by the World Wildlife Fund.

Project area and scope. Thirty-one communities surround the reserves. Monarca, A.C., a nongovernmental organization, began activities in the community adjacent to the reserve by promoting tourism. They also provide information and education on the Monarch butterfly, nationally and internationally.

Region. Thirty-one communities live around the reserves. Because of high population growth, landlessness is becoming increasingly common. Cutbacks at a nearby silver mine have led to a slump in the local economy, increasing the pres-

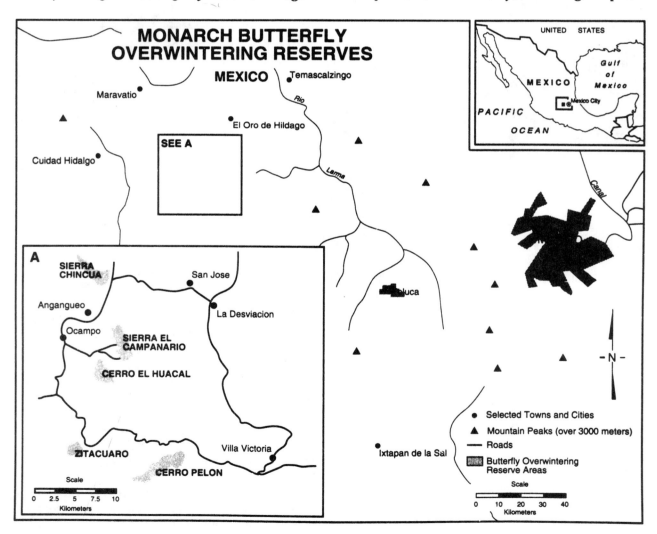

sure on the nearby forests as unemployed workers seek alternative sources of income. Although forestry is the area's economic mainstay, it is inappropriate in many areas because of steep slopes. Most wood is processed outside the region; peasants receive little income from the timber. Subsistence agriculture is prevalent throughout the region, although agricultural production is low because of steep slopes, cold climate, and poor soils. Poverty, scarce economic opportunities, low levels of agricultural production, and increasing population are leading to logging, agriculture, and cattle grazing in the reserves and buffer zones. The reserves are seriously threatened.

Project activities. Monarca, A.C.'s objective has been to protect monarch butterflies. The organization has lobbied for the creation of reserves to protect the monarch's overwintering habitat and has facilitated research on the monarch and its habitat, encouraged the development of a reserve for tourism, developed educational materials and handled public relations about the butterflies, and initiated activities to protect the reserves and work with local communities. Various national and state government agencies, along with Monarca, A.C., developed a plan for integrated development activities in the region to reduce pressure on the reserves. The plan has not been implemented because of a lack of funds or political interest, or both. Tourism is increasing, but this has not provided enough incentive to stop local communities from encroaching on the reserves. Monarca, A.C. has initiated several activities to help one community benefit from tourism. These include helping establish a community store to sell souvenirs to tourists and lobbying to get the community a share of gate receipts. They also have a tree nursery and reforestation program.

Evaluation. Monarca, A.C.'s major accomplishments have been its successful lobbying for the creation of the overwintering reserves and promoting tourism. Its rural development activities have not led to predicted results, however, in part because the scale is too small and Monarca lacks the socioeconomic information needed for project planning and implementation. Although local people receive some tourism revenues, which have been increasing, the revenues have not provided sufficient incentive to halt deforestation. Local people have not been involved in decision-making and no local institutions have been established to manage the tourism. That Monarca, A.C. maintains offices only in Mexico City—to lobby the government and to conduct public relations on the

butterflies and fund-raising—complicates its work in rural areas. The nursery program has had technical problems and has not been able to produce seedlings at expected rates. Threats to the reserves are extremely high and have not been affected by the project. Virtually none of the integrated rural development plan prepared by the government was implemented, and the government has not had any significant enforcement role. Monarca, A.C.'s relationship with the government on reserve management is unclear, but often strained.

Mexico, Sian Ka'an Biosphere Reserve

Protected area. The Sian Ka'an Biosphere Reserve is a 5,230 square kilometer World Heritage site on the eastern side of the Yucatan Peninsula in the state of Quintana Roo. It incorporates tropical forests, mangroves, marshes, and part of the world's second longest barrier reef. Marine and terrestrial areas zoned for total protection make up the core of the reserve (2,400 square kilometers). Buffer zones permitting low-intensity uses, such as tourism and agricultural production, make up the rest. Few threats currently confront the reserve. The greatest problems are lack of government coordination and consequent ineffective management. The reserve management plan has never been officially adopted, leading to speculation that sections of the reserve could be sold and developed for tourism. The turnover rate of park managers and guards has been high.

Projects. Amigos de Sian Ka'an (community development) and the Pilot Forestry Plan (forestry management and processing).

Implementing organization. The Amigos de Sian Ka'an, a nongovernmental organization, was created in 1986 to channel private support into the reserve and to develop and promote sustainable development projects in the region.

Responsible government agency. The State of Quintana Roo and the Ministry of Agriculture and Water Resources initiated the Pilot Forestry Plan project in 1983.

Funding. The World Wildlife Fund provided over $200,000 to Amigos de Sian Ka'an between 1986 and 1990. It is difficult to identify the total funds supporting the Pilot Forestry Plan, although the German government has been a major donor.

Project area and scope. Activities by Amigos de Sian Ka'an are concentrated in several communities in or near the reserve. Pilot Forestry Plan project activities cover approximately 3,000 square kilometers of community forests outside the reserves.

Region. The Sian Ka'an Biosphere Reserve region is one of strong contrasts. Although located in Mexico's fastest growing state, Quintana Roo, there is little evidence of rapid change in the Mayan communities surrounding the biosphere reserve. Most of the growth is concentrated around the tourist resort of Cancun. Approximately 25,000 people live in the communally held peasant landholdings (*ejidos*) surrounding the reserve. Most Mayans on the ejidos are subsistence farmers. Most have retained their language and culture, despite their constant contact with the Hispanic population. Economic pressures are increasingly forcing people, individually or collectively, to cut timber—

to sell or to expand agricultural production. Ejido forests next to the reserve are subject to the greatest pressure. A small community of fishermen (about 1,000 people) live within the reserve and depend on lobster harvesting for their livelihood. The current level of threat to the reserve is low.

Project activities. Amigos de Sian Ka'an has promoted research projects designed to ensure the sustainable harvest of lobster and to preserve palm species used by the fishermen. They have developed a demonstration farm to show the lobster fishermen, who were claiming large tracts of land inside the reserve for agriculture, that adequate production could be achieved on small parcels

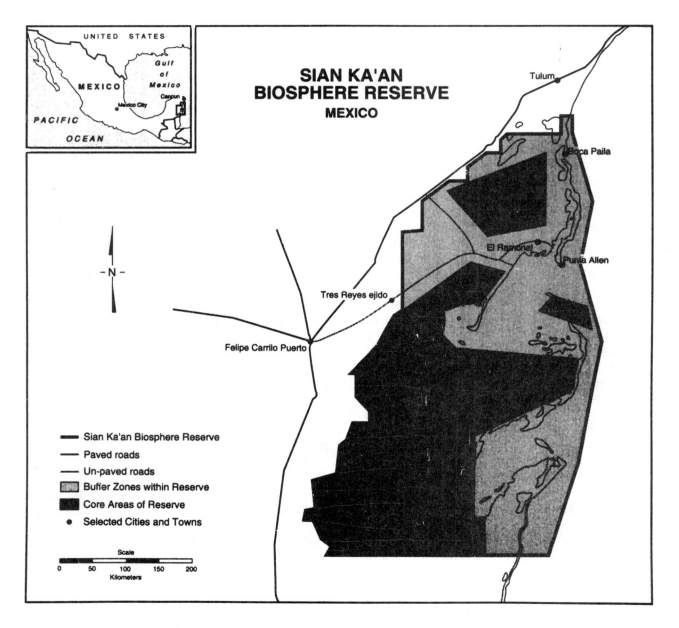

SIAN KA'AN
BIOSPHERE RESERVE
MEXICO

- N -

Legend:
— Sian Ka'an Biosphere Reserve
— Paved roads
— Un-paved roads
▨ Buffer Zones within Reserve
■ Core Areas of Reserve
• Selected Cities and Towns

Scale
0   50   100   150   200
Kilometers

using sustainable agricultural techniques. Amigos de Sian Ka'an has also produced information pamphlets about the reserve and lobbied the government for improved reserve management.

The Pilot Forestry Plan project helps ejidos implement improved forestry practices and diversify forestry industries in the area. The project works with fifty-three ejidos with a population of more than 9,000 families. The forestry potential of each ejido is defined after extensive surveys of forests. A management plan has been developed to guide logging and reforestation. Instead of selling logs to middlemen, the Pilot Forestry Plan helps ejidos increase employment and value added by processing the lumber at the ejido.

Evaluation. The Amigos de Sian Ka'an's rural development activities are small and recent. One project success was that it convinced fishermen to reduce the size of their land claims in the reserve and improve management of the lobster fishery. However, their agricultural intensification project has only been adopted by about fourteen families, and other activities, such as crocodile farming and ecotourism, have yet to show results. Plans for expansion, even if successful, would still be too small to change the surrounding communities enough to affect the reserve. Amigos de Sian Ka'an is working with local communities, but has not developed a strategy for building local institutions. Amigos de Sian Ka'an's relationship to the reserve is unclear; the Mexican government has demonstrated little interest in encouraging local participation or nongovernmental organization involvement in reserve management. Staff turnover has been high and has undoubtedly affected progress, as viewed by both the communities and other agencies involved with the reserve.

As conceived, the Pilot Forestry Plan could have a major effect in maintaining the forest surrounding the Sian Ka'an Biosphere Reserve. Project activities that stress building local capacity, working with established community institutions, and linking development and conservation are too new to have demonstrated positive results.

Peru, Central Selva Region

Protected area. The Central Selva Resource Management project is in the Palcazu Valley, in the central Amazon Rain Forest. The valley lies at the base of the Andes and contains more than a thousand tree species. Elevations in the valley range from 270 meters to 3,800 meters. The 1,220 square kilometer Yanachaga-Chemillen Park was established in 1986

as part of the project. The Yanesha Communal Reserve, which acts as a buffer to the Yanachaga-Chemillen Park, comprises 350 square kilometers of primary forest managed by the Amuesha Indians. The 1,500 square kilometer San Matias-San Carlos Protection Forest provides habitat for endangered animal and plant species, hunting, tourism, scientific research, and related activities.

Project. The Central Selva Resource Management project.

Implementing organizations. The Flora and Fauna Directorate and the Institute for National Development, government of Peru; the Peruvian Foundation for Nature Conservation; the Tropical Science Center; and Amuesha Indian communities.

Responsible government agency. Flora and Fauna Directorate.

Funding. USAID provided $22 million for activities for 1982-87. The Yanesha Forestry Cooperative has received $100,000 from the World Wildlife Fund-U.S. since 1988, when USAID funding ended.

Project area and scope. The project has activities under way in different regions throughout the 140 square kilometer Palcazu Valley (Central Selva).

Region. In 1980, the president of Peru decided that the Central Selva region could be transformed into the country's breadbasket through a large-scale regional development program. This program became known as the Pichis-Palcazu Special project. USAID agreed to fund one component of this project. Land-use studies, however, showed that much of the region was unsuitable for intensive agriculture and that the project would have a negative impact on indigenous peoples. The government of Peru reconsidered its plan, and USAID agreed to support forest management and agroforestry, a protected area component, and local involvement. Conservation units created include Yanachaga-Chemillen Park, the San Matias and San Carlos Protection Forests, and the Yanesha Communal Reserve. When USAID funding ended in 1988, the World Wildlife Fund became involved to support the cooperative and forestry components of the Yanesha Communal Reserve, which belongs to the Amuesha Indians, who have lived in the area for more than a thousand years.

Project activities. In addition to establishing conservation units, the project included an agricultural component to improve farming systems through research, extension, and marketing. Forest production activities, using the strip shelterbelt system, were initiated by the Yanesha Forestry Cooperative, which was formed by the Amuesha. The Amuesha were involved in establishing communal stores, marketing agricultural products, and training for local health and agricultural extension agents. With World Wildlife Fund financing, the project initiated a valleywide forestry extension program, training for members of the cooperative and nonmembers, vehicle purchase, and technical and legal assistance. The cooperative now has more than a hundred members.

Evaluation. By 1987, the Central Selva Resource Management project had realized significant progress, including incorporation of the Yanesha Forestry Cooperative, harvesting of the first two experimental strips, establishment of the national park and protection forests, and identification and mapping of forest production stands. The end of USAID funding and increasing terrorism in the area have seriously limited the project in the past few years, however. Since 1988, activities have been limited to work with the Yanesha Forestry Cooperative, supported by the World Wildlife Fund. The Yanachaga-Chemillen Park remains vulnerable to encroachment from loggers and a proposed road. The initial project design was problematic because local communities were not consulted and the design lacked a strong social component. The project spent a great deal of time trying to compensate for these early design flaws. Although the cooperative has shown some promise, it is still too early to tell whether the strip shelterbelt system and cooperative will be successful. This is especially complicated given the internal problems—both economic and political—that face Peru.

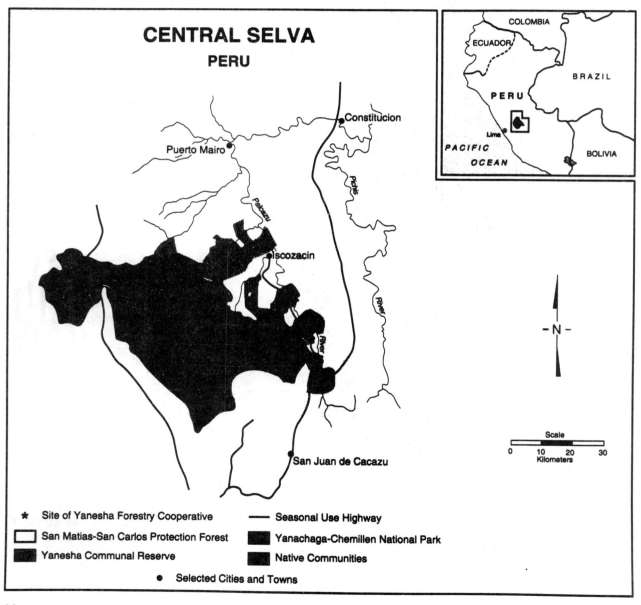

CENTRAL SELVA
PERU

★   Site of Yanesha Forestry Cooperative   ── Seasonal Use Highway

☐   San Matias-San Carlos Protection Forest   ■ Yanachaga-Chemillen National Park

■   Yanesha Communal Reserve   ■ Native Communities

●   Selected Cities and Towns

Bibliography

Annis, S. 1987. "Can small-scale development be a large-scale policy? The case of Latin America." *World Development* 15 (supplement): 129-34.

Batisse, M. 1986. "Developing and focusing the biosphere reserve concept." *Nature and Resources* 22: 1-10.

Boo, E. 1990. *Ecotourism: The potentials and pitfalls.* Washington, D.C.: World Wildlife Fund.

Brandon, K., and M. Wells. 1992. "Planning for people and parks: Design dilemmas." *World Development* forthcoming (April).

Brown, L.D., and D.C. Korten. 1989. "Understanding voluntary organizations: Guidelines for donors." Policy Research Working Paper 258. World Bank, Washington, D.C.

Bunch, R. 1982. *Two ears of corn: A guide to people-centered agricultural improvement.* Oklahoma City, Oklahoma: World Neighbors.

Carruthers, I., and R. Chambers. 1981. "Rapid appraisal for rural development." *Agricultural Administration* 8 (6): 407-22.

Center for International Development and Environment (CIDE) and the National Environment Secretariat (NES), Government of Kenya. 1990. *Participatory rural appraisal handbook.* Natural Resources Management Support Series 1. Washington, D.C.: World Resources Institute.

Cernea, M., ed. 1985. *Putting people first: Sociological variables in rural development.* New York: Oxford University Press.

Cernea, M. 1988a. *Involuntary resettlement in development projects: Policy guidelines in World Bank financed projects.* World Bank Technical Paper 80. Washington, D.C.

Cernea, M. 1988b. *Nongovernmental organizations and local development.* Discussion Paper 40. Washington, D.C.: World Bank.

Chapin, M. "Ecodevelopment and wishful thinking." 1989. *The Ecologist* 19 (Nov./Dec.).

Cohen, J.M., and N.T. Uphoff. 1977. *Rural development participation: Concepts and measures for project design, implementation and evaluation.* Rural Development Committee Monograph 2. Ithaca, New York: Cornell University, Center for International Studies.

Cohen, J.M., and N.T. Uphoff. 1980. "Participation's place in rural development: Seeking clarity through specificity." *World Development* 8: 213-35.

Dixon, J. A., and P.B. Sherman. 1990. *Economics of protected areas: A new look at benefits and costs.* Washington, D.C.: Island Press.

Doolette, J.B., and W.B. Magrath, eds. 1990. *Watershed development in Asia: Strategies and technologies.* World Bank Technical Paper 127. Washington, D.C.

Finnida. 1988. "Amani forest inventory and management plan project: Final report." Helsinki.

Gregersen, H., S. Draper, and D. Elz, eds. 1989. *People and trees: The role of social forestry in sustainable development.* Washington, D.C.: World Bank.

Hales, D. 1989. "Changing concepts of national parks." In D. Western and M. Pearl, eds., *Conservation for the twenty-first century.* New York: Oxford University Press.

Hough, J. 1988a. "Biosphere reserves: Myth and reality." *Endangered Species Update* 6 (1/2): 1-4 (School of Natural Resources, University of Michigan).

———. 1988b. "Obstacles to effective management of conflicts between national parks and surrounding communities in developing countries." *Environmental Conservation* 15 (2): 129-36.

Hough, J., and M.N. Sherpa 1989. "Bottom-up versus basic needs: Integrating conservation and development in the Annapurna and Michiru Mountain Conservation Areas of Nepal and Malawi." *Ambio* 18 (8): 434-41.

International Union for Conservation of Nature and Natural Resources (IUCN). 1980. *World conservation strategy: Living resource conservation for sustainable development.* Gland, Switzerland: IUCN, United Nations Environment Programme, and World Wildlife Fund.

————. 1984. *Threatened protected areas of the world.* Gland, Switzerland: IUCN Commission on National Parks and Protected Areas.

————. 1985. *United Nations list of national parks and protected areas.* Gland, Switzerland.

Jagannathan, N.V. 1989. "Poverty, public policies and the environment." Environment Department Working Paper 24. World Bank, Washington, D.C.

Kiss, A., ed. 1990. *Living with wildlife: Wildlife resource management with local participation in Africa.* Technical Paper 130. Washington, D.C.: World Bank.

Kumar, Krishna. 1987. *Rapid, low-cost data collection methods for A.I.D.* Program Design and Methodology Report 10. Washington, D.C.: U.S. Agency for International Development.

Ledec, G., and R. Goodland. 1988. *Wildlands: Their protection and management in economic development.* Washington, D.C.: World Bank.

Lewis, J.P., ed. 1988. *Strengthening the poor: What have we learned?* U.S.-Third World Policy Perspectives 10. Washington, D.C.: Overseas Development Council.

Lindberg, K. 1991. *Policies for maximizing nature tourism's ecological and economic benefits.* Washington, D.C.: World Resources Institute.

Lusigi, W.J. 1981. "New approaches to wildlife management in Kenya." *Ambio* 10: (2/3): 87-92.

Machlis, G.E., and D.L. Tichnell. 1985. *The state of the world's parks: An international assessment for resource management, policy and research.* Boulder, Colo.: Westview Press.

Mackinnon, J., K. MacKinnon, G. Child, and J. Thorsell. 1986. *Managing protected areas in the tropics.* Gland, Switzerland: International Union for Conservation of Nature and Natural Resources (IUCN).

McCaffrey, D., and H. Landazuri. 1987. *Wildlands and human needs: A program evaluation.* Washington, D.C.: World Wildlife Fund.

McNeely, J.A. 1988. *Economics and biological diversity: Developing and using economic incentives to conserve biological resources.* Gland, Switzerland: International Union for Conservation of Nature and Natural Resources (IUCN).

McNeely, J.A., and K.R. Miller, eds. 1984. *National parks, conservation and development: The role of protected areas in sustaining society.* Washington, D.C.: Smithsonian Institution Press.

McNeely, J.A., K.R. Miller, W.V. Reid, R.A. Mittermeier, and T.B. Werner. 1990. *Conserving the world's biological diversity.* Washington, D.C., and Gland, Switzerland: Conservation International, International Union for Conservation of Nature and Natural Resources (IUCN), World Bank, World Resources Institute, and World Wildlife Fund-U.S.

Midgley, J. 1986. *Community participation, social development and the state.* London: Methuen.

Miller, K.R. 1978. *Planning national parks for ecodevelopment: Methods and cases from Latin America.* Madrid: Fundacion para la Ecologia y Proteccion del Medio Ambiente.

Mishra, H. 1984. "A delicate balance: Tigers, rhinoceros, tourists, and park management vs. the needs of the local people in Royal Chitwan National Park, Nepal." In J.A. McNeely and K.R. Miller, eds., *National parks, conservation and development: The role of protected areas in sustaining society.* Washington, D.C.: Smithsonian Institution Press.

Molnar, A. 1989. *Community forestry: Rapid appraisal.* Community Forestry Note 3. Rome: Food and Agriculture Organization.

Nelson, R. 1988. "Dryland management: The 'desertification' problem." Environment Department Working Paper 8. World Bank, Washington, D.C.

Newby, J. 1990. "Air-Tenere National Park, Niger." In A. Kiss, ed., *Living with wildlife: Wildlife resource management with local participation in Africa.* World Bank Technical Paper 130. Washington, D.C.

Noronha, R. 1980. "Sociological aspects of forestry project design." Agricultural Technical Note 3. World Bank, Washington, D.C.

Oldfield, S. 1988. *Buffer zone management in tropical moist forests: Case studies and guidelines.* Gland, Switzerland: International Union for Conservation of Nature and Natural Resources (IUCN).

Paul, S. 1987. *Community participation in development projects: The World Bank experience.* World Bank Discussion Paper 6. Washington, D.C.

Poole, P. 1989. "Developing a partnership of indigenous peoples, conservationists and land use planners in Latin America." Policy Research Working Paper 245. World Bank, Washington, D.C.

Poore, D., and J. Sayer 1988. *The management of tropical moist forest lands: Ecological guidelines.* Gland, Switzerland: International Union for Conservation of Nature and Natural Resources (IUCN).